FATHERS OF THE BIBLE

FATHERS OF THE BIBLE

ROBERT WOLGEMUTH

ZONDERVAN™

GRAND RAPIDS, MICHIGAN 49530 USA

ZONDERVAN.COM/
AUTHORTRACKER

Fathers of the Bible: A Devotional
Copyright © 2006 by Robert D. Wolgemuth

Requests for information should be addressed to:
Zondervan, *Grand Rapids, Michigan 49530*

Library of Congress Cataloging-in-Publication Data

Wolgemuth, Robert D.
     Fathers of the Bible / Robert Wolgemuth.
        p. cm.
     Adapted from the author's Men of the Bible.
     ISBN-13: 978-0-310-27238-0
     ISBN-10: 0-310-27238-6
     1. Fathers—Prayer-books and devotions—English. 2. Fathers in the
Bible—Meditations. I. Title.
BV4846.S63 2006
220.9'20851—dc22

                                                        2005034026

This edition printed on acid-free paper.

Interior design by Michelle Espinoza

Printed in the United States of America

---

06 07 08 09 10 11 12 • 18 17 16 15 14 13 12 11 10 9 8 7 6 5 4 3 2 1

To
Scott Anderton
Robb Chapin
Mark Oldham
Justin Ramb
David Swanson

Accountable and kind,
Tough and gracious,
Sober and uproarious.
Men who know God,
And seek to know him more.
Husbands, fathers, friends.

— Robert Wolgemuth

CONTENTS

"THIS BABY IS YOURS, DAD"

What does it take to become a father?

As young boys, we have all had an unforgettable conversation that unlocked the physiological — the mechanical — answer to the question: "Where do babies come from?" We couldn't have possibly been prepared for the answer. An older brother, a neighbor boy, someone at school, or perhaps a cousin filled us in on the amazing — and unthinkable — details. Of course, most parents want to be the first ones to disclose this sensitive information to their children.

They rarely are.

Many years have passed since you and I first learned about how these things work. And they *do* work. Witness the fact that we're fathers. And we know full well that being a dad is a whole lot more than the mechanics of the intimate. It's much bigger than the contribution of our chromosomes to a quiet and miraculous transaction in the darkness of our baby's mother's body.

On the day that you and I became fathers, we knew that our lives were about to unalterably change. Someone handed us a tiny child, topped with a knit cap, tucked together and wrapped like a warm burrito. We heard the words, "This baby is yours, Dad." Our hearts pounded with a staggering mix of wonder and fear. *Wonder* because of the intricate details of each wrinkle and fold ... the dark eyes trying to open and focus ... the tiny hands ... the fragile stratum of velvet fuzz that covered their skin ... the cheeks so kissable, an invitation to which we enthusiastically replied.

"Beautiful" doesn't come close.

And we were *fearful* because of the weighty responsibility that was ours. We became the father. (If you adopted your baby, you still remember this moment.) The only one this child would ever have. We would be called on to lead and counsel where we had no training. To listen and comfort where our instincts surely called for something else. To discipline and model in places where *we* had failed.

So where does a dad turn? Where does he go for help he can count on?

Sadly, a baby comes without instructions ... not that we would have read them anyway.

I have good news. Actually, I have *great* news. God knows about being a father, and he's more than willing to show us what to do.

Before time began, there was a Father, a Son, and a Holy Spirit. Although this is a difficult truth to fully understand, God was — and is — three distinct persons ... yet he is still One. And in his sovereign plan, he chose a model — a relationship — that you and I would understand. A dad, a kid, and an invisible and unassailable spirit that binds them together. Forever.

So, when you and I take a Bible in our hands, we are actually holding a user's manual for a father. Page after page, story after story, we read how this Father loves his Son ... and us, his Son's brothers and sisters. This holy Book reveals:

- the firmness of his discipline and the tenderness of his grace
- the visible command of his spoken word and the mysterious power of his whisper

- the heart-breaking results of his indignation and the comforting assurance of his enfolding arms

Just like a father.

And woven throughout Scripture are the historical accounts of other fathers—earthly dads. Some are exemplary, others not so. Some set an example worthy of duplicating. Others lay down a marker to be avoided at all costs.

The following twelve chapters offer a slice of the biblical accounts of men who were fathers—their accomplishments, their fears, their victories, and their pain. From each we can learn something important about the tasks, the privileges, the challenges, and the failures of fatherhood. We'll discover the faithfulness of Noah, the conniving of Jacob, the unbridled passion of David, and the quiet confidence of Joseph, the man God chose to be the earthly father of Jesus.

Each of these men were dads. Their geographic settings and life circumstances were vastly different from yours and mine, but the struggles and challenges of fatherhood, remarkably similar. We have something important to learn from each one.

The format of this book gives you the chance to spend ten or fifteen minutes a day for one week with each of these—twelve weeks of understanding. However you decide to space these out is up to you. Here you'll be able to examine the examples they set for us to follow, or to run from. You will study the lessons to be learned from their experiences. And together we'll capture biblical themes that provide direction and encouragement as we face the predictable rigors of the mission ahead.

The goal here is to find something in these stories that quickens our own walk with God and informs our unique charge as dads — encouragement and guidance we can put to use right away. This baby is yours, Dad.

Welcome.

Dr. Robert Wolgemuth
Orlando, Florida

HOW TO USE THIS BOOK

There are twelve chapters in this book, each focused on a biblical father. Of course, you are welcome to use it however you choose. But when I put it together, my plan was that you would spend an entire week "soaking" in the story of each of these men. You can do this by yourself, or with a small group of friends.

To help you better understand and experience their stories, we have developed a unique devotional program, combining five elements: inspiration, character examination, Bible study, fathering insight, Bible promises, and prayer. Here's how each of the twelve weeks unfolds, focusing on a particular dad in the Bible:

Monday: His Story—a portrait of one father's life.
Tuesday: A Look at the Man—a closer look into his character.
Wednesday: His Legacy in Scripture—a short Bible study on his life with application for yourself.
Thursday: His Legacy as a Father—a snapshot at his fathering and Bible promises that apply to his life and yours.
Friday: His Legacy of Prayer—praying in light of his story.

By focusing on one father for five consecutive days, we hope to help you read, reflect, study, and pray in a way that will draw you more deeply into God's presence, experiencing his grace as you live out your own call to fatherhood.

You know that being a dad is one of the most difficult and rewarding challenges in the world. We hope that *Fathers of the Bible* will offer you an opportunity alone or with a group of friends to experience God's love and faithfulness in fresh ways, blessing your children through the work he does in your life.

I owe special thanks to associate publisher Sandy Vander Zicht, for her continuing insight, encouragement, and advocacy for this book. Every author needs an in-house champion — in Sandy that's exactly what I have. I am also grateful to Verlyn Verbrugge for his crisp editorial help, to creative director Cindy Davis in the design of the book, and to Zondervan's marketing and sales teams around the world for their hard work in making it available to as many readers as possible, including you.

ADAM

His Name Means *Of the Ground*

❦

His Children: Cain, Abel, Seth

His Work: Until his sin, Adam was naked and was the happy caretaker of the Garden of Eden. After succumbing to temptation, he tailored his own clothes and became a farmer.

His Character: The first man, Adam, was initially God's perfect human creation. Adam was in harmony with nature and with his wife, Eve, who was formed from one of his ribs.

His Sorrow: More tragic than any story in the Bible, Adam disobeyed God, was expelled from the garden of Eden, and spent the rest of his life in hard labor.

His Triumph: Adam was the firstborn of all creation.

Key Scriptures: Genesis 2–3

HIS STORY

"What's that sound?" The tension in Eve's voice reflected the new feelings in Adam's gut. His mind and heart swirled with sickening sensations, ones he wished he had never experienced, born of deepest guilt and the terror of truth.

Until this moment, his life had been filled with remarkable delight.

It all began when Adam took his first breath.

The span of time between morning consciousness and gathering enough energy to open one's eyes usually takes just a few moments. But for Adam, the prewaking experience of semiconsciousness must have taken some time. This was unlike anything that had ever happened before—or has happened since: a full-grown man literally sucking in his first gulp of air.

As he lay somewhere between sleep and full consciousness, Adam's first thoughts must have been, *Who am I? What are those sounds? Where am I? What is this?*

Brushing the sleep from his eyes, accepting life, Adam slowly sat up. He looked down at his own legs and arms and saw smooth skin and firm, strong muscles. He lifted his hands to his face, bending and stretching his fingers, studying the sinews. He drew his hands closer and touched his face, feeling the contours of his eyes and cheekbones, then briefly touched his hair, thick and long.

Adam slowly stood to his feet. He tightened the muscles of his legs and stretched his new arms skyward. He drew in a deep breath of fresh, cool air that would rival a pristine, deep forest breath. And it was only then that Adam saw something of the breathtaking beauty that surrounded him.

The foliage was lush, the flowers a panoply of color. The fully orchestrated sounds of songbirds and animals filled his head with sheer ecstasy. *I am alive.* He took another deep breath. *Life is good.*

Adam began to walk. Slowly at first, then a jog, finally a dead run. Like a child turned loose, the man finally pulled up and spun around, his arms spread wide. He sang and shouted sounds from his own mouth, something he had never heard before.

And if the sounds and the beauty and the wind tousling his hair were not enough to flood his senses, Adam felt an indescribable Presence. Yes, there were lots of living things around him, but this was different—an inexpressible Someone. All about him. Over there ... over there ... and over there. Whoever it was, Adam inherently knew that he was not the only one in the garden. Yet he was not afraid; instead, he was comforted by the Presence.

Adam stopped in a small meadow, the soft grass cushioning his feet. The glowing yellow sun in the sky warmed his shoulders. He looked at the trees surrounding him and felt a vague emptiness in the pit of his stomach.

And then, for the first time, Adam heard a voice, a sound different from the sound of any of the other living things around him. He heard words—a language that took shape and became immediate knowledge in his mind. The voice was quiet and authoritative, and he recognized it as belonging to the Presence.

"You are free to eat from any tree in the garden," the voice said, "but you must not eat from the tree of the knowledge of good and evil, for when you eat of it you will surely die."

Adam nodded his willing compliance. He noted the tree to his left and decided he was more than willing to obey. *With all of this*, he thought, looking all about, *why would I miss the fruit of that tree? It's an easy promise.*

Walking to a small bush covered with red fruit, Adam pulled a berry from a reluctant stem and tentatively bit into it. Juice covered his tongue and ran down his throat, tickling his mouth with a delightful sweet-tart sensation. Eagerly, he gathered others and shoved them into his mouth.

Then from the woods and skies, animals and birds approached him. As though mysteriously commanded to organize, these living things passed by, and group by group, Adam called out their names. And once they were named, they scattered again.

If ever a man experienced satisfaction by his surroundings, it was Adam. There was the invisible Presence, the creatures, the vegetation, and the fruit. But they weren't enough. Deep in his soul, Adam longed for something—or someone—else by his side.

"It is not good for you to be alone," the voice spoke again. "I will make a helper suitable for you."

Adam sat down. The words warmed him. He knew that the Presence understood his longing.

First a drowsiness, then a complete fatigue overwhelmed Adam. He laid his head on the soft grass and closed his eyes.

In what seemed like a moment, he slowly opened his eyes, snatching consciousness from the mist of sleep. As his eyes took focus, he saw a form lying on the ground next to him. His heart raced at the beauty of the creature, like him in some ways, different in delightful other ways.

Rising to his feet, Adam took the hand of the woman, helping her to stand. Their eyes met. They smiled and gently extended their arms toward each other until they embraced. Feeling the warmth of her body against his own, Adam nestled his face on the woman's neck. And her presence filled the hollowness in his heart. A perfect companion.

Adam felt an unexplainable sense of completeness. Wholeness. This was someone with whom he could share the beauty and company of the garden. Joy filled him and spilled upward, causing him to smile.

"I'm Adam," he said.

She smiled with a silent understanding.

"And you're Eve."

Taking her hand once more, Adam walked with her into the woods. He spoke of his own "birth," the parade of living things, the taste of the fruit, and the beauty of their surroundings. Adam told her of the Presence and how she was the perfect answer to his yearning.

But this pristine perfection would come to a dreadful end. As time went on, something happened. Something awful. What should have been enough became clouded with a new longing. It started with an innocent conversation with a serpent and a fascination with that forbidden tree. Whispers of untold pleasure and desire. Conspiracy between man and woman to blatantly disobey the Presence.

Now new feelings of fear and dread engulfed Adam's soul, eating away the peace and joy that once lived there. And when he and his mate heard the Presence—the sovereign Creator—walking in the garden, they instinctively cowered, ducking behind the brush.

Shame filled them, flushing their faces with heat, widening their eyes with fear at what was to come. The Presence. Judgment.

"What's that sound?" Eve whispered again.

But they both knew exactly who it was and why he had come.

A LOOK AT THE MAN

For the Man Who Has Everything

Try to imagine what it must have been like to wake up for the first time as a grown man—to rub the sleep from your eyes and not know anything about anything. This is exactly what happened to Adam. Everything was unfamiliar and new. His mind must have spun with possible scenarios of who he was and who put him in the garden.

The first few days of Adam's life were an indescribable sequence of extrasensory experiences, like checking into one of those opulent European hotels, all expenses paid—only much better and much more extravagant. Everywhere he turned he saw lavish beauty. And because no other man was in sight, Adam rightly assumed that all of this belonged to him.

And if that wasn't enough, Adam's great longing—for perfect human companionship—was completely satisfied with the creation of a woman, her face lovely and radiant, her companionship pleasing, her affection for him alone.

Every day the Life section of *USA Today* tells of the rich and famous, the accomplished and gifted, the successful and powerful—the beautiful people. But if ever there was such a person, Adam was surely the man who had everything. How could he possibly want for more?

But, incredibly, he did want more. He refused to be satisfied with what God had provided for his pleasure. His heart was piqued with a hint of discontent. He wanted to go his own way, to do what he wanted to do, to be his own man.

And so the only thing God had told him to avoid became the very thing he submitted to. Willing to sacrifice his abundance on the altar of this temptation, Adam, the man who had absolutely everything, lost absolutely everything. All of this ruin over a silly bite of fruit he was told to avoid. What a foolish wager! What a waste of paradise!

The man who has it all risks it all on something shameful and inconsequential. But doesn't this sound strangely familiar? Of course it does. Every once in a while the beautiful people in the Life section find their way to the News section — indicted for shoplifting, embezzlement, fraud, assault, and even murder. And so, by their own accord, they exchange their riches for the poverty of embarrassment and exile — a page right out of Genesis 3.

But before we jump to judgment against Adam and these fallen contemporary heroes, we have our own hearts to deal with, don't we? Our longing for more when we have enough. Our sin of discontent in the midst of plenty.

HIS LEGACY IN SCRIPTURE

Read Genesis 1:26–28

1. Why do you think God made men and women in his image? What does it mean to bear God's image?
2. God told the first human beings to fill the earth and subdue it. What might that have involved before the fall? What about after the fall?

Read Genesis 2:15–24

3. What role does obedience play when it comes to enjoying the good God intends for us? Think of instances in your own life that have required obedience. How have you experienced God's goodness during such times?
4. God saw that Adam was incomplete without a partner. And Adam seemed delighted by the woman God made for him. When married couples blend their lives to do God's will, God's initial plan is carried forward. What makes couples who have a strong marriage so effective and happy?

Going Deeper: Read Genesis 3:8–24

5. Why did Adam and Eve suddenly become aware of their nakedness after they disobeyed God? What did

their attempt to make clothing for themselves from the skins of animals signify?

6. Why did they hide from God? Think about ways you tend to "hide from God" when you do something wrong.

HIS LEGACY AS A FATHER

Adam's story offers a glimpse of the good life God intended for all of us. He was the first to commune with God, the first to look at everything beautiful, the first to enjoy an intimate relationship with his wife, the first to be given satisfying work at which he could certainly succeed … and the first dad. And until he made the mistake of a lifetime, utter peace, perfect health, supreme confidence were his.

Unfortunately, Adam, along with Eve, was also the first to lead the way into sin — into that dark tunnel full of misery and death. And this became the legacy he passed on to his children: Cain, Abel, Seth … you and me.

Still, Adam retained his status as a creature made in God's image, even though that image became suddenly distorted. Thankfully centuries later, God initiated a plan to restore his image in the children of Adam (that's us) by making us the children of the new Adam (that's Christ).

And through an intimate friendship with Jesus Christ, who sacrificed himself as did the animals that clothed Adam and Eve with the sacrifice of their own lives, our legacy as fathers can be one that demonstrates God's sacrificial love and grace. Even though we are as sinful as Adam, our homes have an opportunity to be the sacred garden where Adam first lived. Because, in Christ, all things are new.

Promises in Scripture

For as in Adam all die, so in Christ all will be made alive.

—1 Corinthians 15:22

Therefore, if anyone is in Christ, he is a new creation; the old has gone, the new has come!

—2 Corinthians 5:17

Because of the LORD's great love we are not consumed,
for his compassions never fail.
They are new every morning;
great is your faithfulness.

—Lamentations 3:22–23

"Where, O death, is your victory?
Where, O death, is your sting?"

The sting of death is sin, and the power of sin is the law. But thanks be to God! He gives us the victory through our Lord Jesus Christ.

—1 Corinthians 15:55–57

HIS LEGACY OF PRAYER

The LORD God took the man and put him in the Garden of Eden to work it and take care of it. And the LORD God commanded the man, "You are free to eat from any tree in the garden; but you must not eat from the tree of the knowledge of good and evil, for when you eat of it you will surely die."

—Genesis 2:15 – 17

Reflect On: Genesis 2:8 – 25.

Praise God: For creating you in his own image.

Offer Thanks: For the task God has given you as a father. And thank him for his grace, giving you a chance to follow Christ and lead your children as a forgiven man.

Confess: Any discontent, disobedience, or mistrust that prevents you from enjoying the good things God intends for your life.

Ask God: To help you understand the link between obedience and blessing.

Every day offers us another chance. Either we can become more like Adam, the natural man who follows his own independent course, or we can become more like Christ, the supernatural man who selflessly depends on God for everything in his life. Take a few minutes today to slow down and ask yourself where God is requiring your obedience. Maybe he wants you to look for a new job, to keep putting up with your old job, to spend more time with your children, or to get help with a persistent sin. Whatever it is, don't hide from the truth, but face it, trusting that if God is showing it to you, he will help you make the change and bless you in the process.

Heavenly Father, you know how hard it is for me to rely on anyone but myself. I don't like the idea of depending on someone else. Help me, God, to learn how to trust and obey you no matter how "unnatural" it may feel. Help me to remember the example of my brother, Jesus, who depended on you for everything and who never once went his own way. In his name I pray, Amen.

NOAH

His Name Means *To Rest*

⁘

His Children: Shem, Ham, Japheth

His Work: We don't know what Noah did for a living before he heard from God, but following that encounter, he became an accomplished carpenter.

His Character: Noah was a righteous man, obedient and faithful.

His Sorrow: In spite of his admonitions and warnings, Noah was unable to convince his neighbors, friends, and extended family to repent. As a result, they were all drowned in the flood.

His Triumph: Noah's obedience saved not only his life but the lives of his wife and children.

Key Scriptures: Genesis 6 – 7

HIS STORY

The sound of muffled weeping awakened the woman. Reaching out, she gently touched her husband's shoulder. Moving her body close to his, she held him until the sobbing subsided.

No words were spoken. No explanation was necessary. Over the years, she had slowly watched her husband become isolated from his family and friends. His righteous life was enough to keep him at arm's length from most people. But he had "heard God's voice" and undertaken the most massive—and ridiculous—building project anyone had ever seen. Her husband had built an enormous boat—in their backyard.

She had questioned him many times, gently at first, then more and more pointedly as the years had passed. Frankly, this undertaking had been an embarrassment to her and their sons. But in time she had learned to trust her husband and their God, and so she had supported and loved Noah.

Tonight she held him close as she had through the years and years of frustration and fear and wakeful nights. This time, however, the methodical rocking motion of the boat in which they were lying brought them welcomed sleep.

From the time his father, Lamech, had told him of the immortal God and the need to live righteously, Noah had sought to be obedient and to follow the God of his father. Most of the time, Noah could ignore the derision and segregation from others — others who noted his loyalty to God's ways and hated him for it. But sometimes the loneliness became too much to bear, especially during the solitude of the night.

Nine generations had passed since Eden. The unsullied garden and the flawless world surrounding it had become a cesspool of debauchery and sin. Violence, corruption, and sexual lewdness were not only commonplace but were so prevalent they were going unnoticed — except by the mournful eye of the Creator himself.

Early one day as Noah walked through the morning mist, he heard the voice of God. There had been other times when Noah had sensed or felt the voice of the Lord, but this time was different. This time God's voice was audible and clear — and his words were shocking.

"I am going to put an end to all people, for the earth is filled with violence because of them. I am surely going to destroy both them and the earth." Then the Lord laid out his plan to his servant, who cowered in fear at God's awful words and crazy directions. "Collect your tools ... gather supplies ... and build a boat. A very big boat. I am going to bring floodwaters on the earth to destroy all life under the heavens, every creature that has the breath of life in it. Everything on earth will perish."

Noah struggled to comprehend such a thought. Total destruction of the earth? But God wasn't finished. God instructed Noah to collect two of every kind of bird and animal and to place them in the boat along with his family.

Completely dazed by what he had just heard but determined to be obedient, Noah did everything just as God commanded him.

But as the days melted into weeks and the weeks into months ... and the months into years, Noah grew tired. The physical labor took its toll on the man, but the incessant mocking from many whom he had once called friends found a foothold in his soul.

"What's the matter, Noah?" they jeered. "Did you forget that you live in the desert? How are you going to get that monstrosity to the sea?"

"Have you gone mad?"

Noah wondered if they were right. But over and over, he went back to the words he had heard from God, determined to remain true to his original mission.

Decades passed, and finally the work was finished. Built to God's precise specifications, the ark was ready for its occupants —and the flood.

Diligently Noah collected two of every creature, shepherding them into the craft. Finally, the ominous task was complete. Each living thing nestled in its rightful cubicle in the massive boat. Noah's ark rose from the desert floor like a great and mighty monument to his obedience.

Then the Lord spoke to his faithful servant, "Go into the ark, you and your whole family, because I have found you righteous in this generation.... Seven days from now I will send rain on the earth for forty days and forty nights, and I will wipe from the face of the earth every living creature I have made."

Finally, once everyone—including Noah's own precious children—was on board, the Lord shut him in.

And the rains fell.

Noah's neighbors and friends and cousins died, groping for air, some clinging to the boat until they could no longer hold on. Every single one was drowned and gone, suffocated by the swirling deep.

And in the darkness of the night, aboard a massive, noisy ship floating on an endless sea, the thought of this brought Noah to tears.

A LOOK AT THE MAN

All Aboard

Once in a while a man comes along who's not afraid to obey.

We cannot imagine what it must have been like to be Noah. He lived in a culture that was corrupted by immorality and violence. According to the story, the earth was literally "full" of it.

So reprehensible were people's lives that God regretted having created these divine image-bearers. So much so that he decided to remove every living thing from the face of the earth, like a man clearing a table with the back of his hand. Can you imagine?

But on his way to starting all over again, the Lord took a second look at Noah. His life as a man, a husband, and father was so exemplary that in the middle of all this debauchery, he found favor in God's eyes. This man, Noah, was righteous and blameless among the people of his time. Because of his faithfulness, he was the one man whom the Lord chose not to destroy.

We don't have to look very far to find a lesson in this man's life. Like Noah's culture, the one that surrounds us and our families is drowning in immorality, corruption, and violence. And like Noah, we can choose to quietly capitulate or to stand against it. Once we decide to stand firm — to live in obedience to God — the tricky part comes with trying to understand how. What does submission to him look like? And what should we expect as the result of this obedience?

Tucked away in this story is the secret to Noah's success. Noah "walked with God." For Noah, surrender was not a single decision or noteworthy event; it was a process. A routine. A journey. A walk. Obedience was the natural result of this methodical approach. Walking with God meant knowing him. Knowing God meant loving him. Loving meant hearing. Hearing, obeying.

And obeying God meant salvation.

We can imagine that decades of subtle and overt ridicule may have led Noah to question God. There had to have been moments of loneliness and genuine doubt. But taking one step at a time along the path God had laid out for him kept Noah on track.

Noah's obedience led to the preservation of not only his own life, but of the lives of his wife and children as well. Once the project was complete and everyone around him had rejected the notion that God would actually destroy the earth with a catastrophic flood, Noah and his whole family entered the safety of the ark. Then the Lord shut him in.

In fact, Noah's faithfulness—in the form of a great ark —became one of the early church's symbols for refuge. The interiors of many great cathedrals were built to resemble the inside of a boat—a shelter in the time of storm, a reminder of an obedient man who went before us and was saved.

HIS LEGACY IN SCRIPTURE

Read Genesis 6:5 – 22

1. How do you think God feels when we distort his image in us by our selfishness, greed, and violence? Do you think God is injured by sin? Why or why not?

2. Put yourself in Noah's place (vv. 9 – 11). What does it feel like to follow God even though everyone around you is heading in the opposite direction?

3. God did not completely destroy the world but carried out a plan to renew it. What does this say about his mercy? How can you reflect mercy to those who are not living for God?

4. God saved not only Noah but his wife, his sons, and their wives. What does this say about the way God's blessings work within a family? How have you experienced God blessing your own family?

Read Genesis 9:8 – 16

5. God promised to "remember" his covenant whenever a rainbow appeared in the clouds. "To remember" in the Bible refers not simply to recalling something but to being concerned for or caring for it. How does Noah's story speak about God's care for the world after the flood?

Interesting Observation on Genesis 5

It's tempting to dismiss genealogies in Scripture as long, boring lists of unfamiliar names. But careful reading often yields interesting insights. Keep in mind that the most important names in any biblical genealogy are usually the first and the last, in this case Adam and Noah (along with his sons). The meaning of Noah's name is connected to ideas of "rest" or "bringing relief." When Noah's father named him (v. 29), he associated the name with relief from the curse originally placed on Adam.

Interesting Observation on Genesis 8:11

Olive trees grow only at lower altitudes. When the dove returned to the ark with a freshly plucked olive leaf in its beak, Noah realized how far the water had receded. The dove with an olive branch in its beak has become a universally recognized symbol of peace.

HIS LEGACY AS A FATHER

The story of Noah is one of the most amazing in the Bible. It may also be the most frequently used story in church school classes for small children. But don't be misled—this man wasn't just some sticker-book hero for little kids. Noah was a man of God and a dad from whom we can learn a lot.

Because of the awful wickedness of the culture in which he lived, God pronounced judgment. However, that judgment did not fall on Noah—and for good reason. "Noah found favor in the eyes of the LORD" (Genesis 6:8). And Noah "walked with God" (Genesis 6:9). God's grace coupled with Noah's faithfulness spelled salvation.

As fathers, the message for you and me is found in Genesis 7:1. God said to Noah, "Go into the ark, you and your whole family, because I have found you righteous in this generation."

We have been given different assignments. We may be doctors, farmers, salesmen, executives, laborers, brokers, or ship builders. But two of the tasks he has delivered are the same for you and me. We are to (1) walk with him, and we are to (2) bring our families along.

Promises in Scripture

> *Whenever the rainbow appears in the clouds, I will see it and remember the everlasting covenant between God and all living creatures of every kind on the earth.*
>
> —Genesis 9:16

There is a future for the man of peace.

—Psalm 37:37

"Though the mountains be shaken
and the hills be removed,
yet my unfailing love for you will not be shaken
nor my covenant of peace be removed,"
says the LORD, who has compassion on you.

—Isaiah 54:10

HIS LEGACY OF PRAYER

Noah found favor in the eyes of the LORD.... Noah was a righteous man, blameless among the people of his time, and he walked with God.

—Genesis 6:8–9

Reflect On: Genesis 8.

Praise God: For using his followers to accomplish his purposes.

Offer Thanks: For God's mercy toward the human race.

Confess: Any tendency to care more about what the world thinks of you than about what God thinks.

Ask God: To show you what it means, not just to obey a set of laws, but to stay close to him throughout your life—to walk with him.

What would have happened had Noah not found favor with God, if his heart had been as wayward as every other man's? Would God have spared the human race even though he couldn't find a single person worth saving? Or would the human world simply have vanished? End of story. Finis. Caput.

Noah's experience of God reminds us of the importance of one good life. No matter how difficult it may be to remain faithful, no matter how insignificant your life may sometimes seem, no life is small in God's sight. It doesn't matter what your natural gifts are or how much money you make or how fit you seem or how clever you may be. God looks at your heart. Nothing else. If he finds his own reflection there, he will use you — and it will surprise you to realize someday just how powerfully his grace has been at work through you, transforming your family, your work, and the world around you.

Lord, give me the courage to follow you even when those around me are heading in another direction. Help me to stay close to you, not walling you out of my life but inviting you in. Help me to listen for your voice. Please make quick obedience the core of my character. Use me in ways that will help others to celebrate your faithfulness. Amen.

ABRAHAM

His Name Means *Father of a Multitude*

～❧～

His Children: Ishmael, Isaac, Midian, Zimran, Jokshan, Medan, Ishbak, and Shuah

His Work: A tender of livestock.

His Character: Abraham was a man of faith who followed God even in the most challenging of circumstances.

His Sorrow: At times Abraham compromised God's instructions.

His Triumph: Abraham obeyed God, and God blessed him with a son in his old age.

Key Scriptures: Genesis 12 – 23

HIS STORY

One by one, Abraham took the pieces of wood he had cut, stacking them on his young son's back. Then he slipped his knife into his belt, took the torch from his servant, and began walking up the steep slope of the mountain—just he and his boy.

Then, almost as an afterthought, he turned and said to his servants as they prepared to follow, "We will worship and then we will come back to you."

Abraham and Isaac walked along in silence. Since they had left on their journey three days before, Isaac could tell that something was troubling his father. The spontaneity and camaraderie that marked their relationship was gone. Conversation had seemed strained and wooden.

Unknown to Isaac, the day before they left home, God had ordered Abraham to sacrifice Isaac as a burnt offering on one of the mountains. Abraham's quiet spirit at the awful assignment was unbearable. He had waited a lifetime for this son. Now God was asking the most terrible sacrifice a man could imagine, a sacrifice that seemed to contradict the promise God had made so many years before, to give him a son and heir, to make of him a nation uniquely blessed.

Along the journey, Isaac hadn't had the courage to ask if anything was wrong. In fact, something told him that this awkward silence had something to do with him, so it was best left unexplored. He'd learn soon enough.

"Father?" Isaac finally said as they made their way up the trail.

"Yes, my son?"

"The fire and wood are here ... but where is the lamb for the burnt offering?"

Like spears, Isaac's words must have plunged themselves into Abraham, deepening his distress — even panic — but he wasn't going to let his son in on any notion of uncertainty. Mustering all the courage he could, Isaac's father spoke. "God himself will provide."

When the man and his son reached the spot God had told Abraham about, they stopped. Propping the burning torch against a rock, he took the wood from Isaac's back and carefully laid it out over a heap of stones to form an altar. Neither of them spoke, but the emotion of the moment must have been overwhelming. *God himself will provide. God himself will provide. God himself will provide.* The cadence of this assurance repeated itself in Abraham's mind as he put the wood in place.

Pulling the strap from his sandal, Abraham nodded toward his only son. Silently and without resistance, the boy stepped forward. With the leather string, Abraham tied his son's hands together and lifted him onto the altar.

Did God not promise? Abraham must have reviewed God's pledge as he removed his knife from its sheath. *"Your wife Sarah will bear you a son.... I will establish my covenant with him for his descendants after him."* And then he must have wondered, *How can this be if this covenant son is dead?*

Extending his arm above the boy, Abraham lifted the knife, ready to plunge it into the chest of his precious son.

God himself will provide, Abraham breathed one last time.

"Abraham! Abraham!" The words from an emissary of the sovereign God literally shook the ground.

"Here I am," Abraham responded. His arm did not move.

"Do not lay a hand on the boy.... Do not do anything to him."

The sinews in Abraham's arm released as it collapsed to his side, the knife dropping harmlessly to the ground.

"Now I know that you fear God, because you have not withheld from me your son, your only son."

At that moment, Abraham looked and saw a ram that had tangled its horns in a thicket. He walked to the bush, released the ram, and brought it back to the altar. Picking up his knife, Abraham cut the strap that had bound Isaac.

The boy crawled down from the altar as his father laid the ram on the same spot where Isaac had just been lying. Pulling the sharp knife across the animal's throat, Abraham and Isaac watched as the ram's blood spilled down the wood and onto the ground.

Emotion welled up in Abraham's soul. He wrapped his arms around his boy. God had indeed provided.

Once again God's messenger spoke in an audible voice. "Because you have done this and have not withheld your son, your only son, I will surely bless you and make your descendants as numerous as the stars in the sky and as the sand on the seashore.... All nations on earth will be blessed, because you have obeyed me."

When the sacrifice was finished, the final embers extinguished, Abraham and his son descended the mountain.

Going down a hill is always easier than climbing up, but without the burden of the wood and the anguish of heart, the ease of the downward slope was even more wonderful. Abraham's obedience would be bountifully rewarded.

A LOOK AT THE MAN

God Will Provide

The life of Abraham is a study in faithfulness, obedience, and sometimes blind trust. It's also the story of a God who keeps his covenant promises.

Abram (later named Abraham) and his wife Sarai (later named Sarah) lived in Haran where Abraham was a prosperous livestock owner. By all accounts, he was comfortable. But an order from the living God changed all that.

"Leave your country, your people and your father's household and go to the land I will show you." God did not mince his words. He didn't even ask Abraham to consider moving. He *told* him to go. And to make it even more of a challenge, God didn't specify Abraham's destination. He only said, "Go." And then God made Abraham a promise. "I will make you into a great nation and I will bless you."

It's hard to imagine how shocking this news was to Abraham. And when Sarah heard Abraham's report of what God had said, she must have been overwhelmed. "Leave our home? Go on a journey to nowhere? Have children even though we are old and barren?"

But Sarah trusted Abraham, just as Abraham trusted God. They said good-bye to their families and, along with their nephew, Lot, their possessions, and a caravan of servants, they set out southwest toward Canaan, the area Abraham's descendants would call "home" to this day.

Time and again, throughout his life, God tested Abraham's resolve to obey him. And, time and again, God reconfirmed his promise to Abraham — a land, a son, a nation, and a blessing.

Abraham is the most revered of the patriarchs. His name and God's promise of a nation were even remembered as Mary accepted her call to be the mother of Jesus. "God has helped his servant Israel, not forgetting to be merciful to Abraham and his descendants forever even as he promised."

But Abraham's place in history is not only well established because of the millions who count themselves as his offspring. Nor is Abraham honored because he was a perfect man. He wasn't.

Abraham is the most significant patriarch because of God's call and covenant with him and Abraham's remarkable courage to be obedient.

HIS LEGACY IN SCRIPTURE

Read Genesis 22:1

1. What did it mean for Abraham to be "tested" by God? When have you ever felt that God might be testing you? How did you respond?

Read Genesis 17:15–16 and Genesis 22:2

2. By commanding Abraham to sacrifice his "only son," "the son whom you love," God seemed to be both emphasizing the difficulty of what he was asking and contradicting the promise he had made to Abraham. When have you ever had difficulty believing God's promises? What in Abraham's story can help you believe and obey God regardless of your circumstances?

Read Genesis 22:6–8 and John 19:16–18

3. Compare these passages. How many similarities can you find between the story of Abraham and Isaac and the story of God and Jesus?

Read Genesis 22:9–14, 16–18

4. Put yourself in Abraham's place. Consider how difficult his obedience must have been. Then consider his relief and joy as Isaac is spared. How has God's provision affected your life?

5. Faith runs along the lines of God's promises. In other words, our faith will not be disappointed if we put it to work in connection with the promises God has clearly made. But God's promises often have conditions attached to them. How is that evident in Abraham's story?

Interesting Fact

Moriah signifies the "place of provision of Yahweh." Though scholars have not been able to identify the exact location of the mountain where Abraham brought his son to be sacrificed, some ancient sources identify it with a site in Jerusalem on which the Dome of the Rock (a Moslem mosque) currently sits (see 2 Chronicles 3:1). Interestingly, the Dome of the Rock, located on the Temple Mount, is just a few hundred yards from the Church of the Holy Sepulchre, traditionally identified as the site of Jesus' crucifixion.

HIS LEGACY AS A FATHER

Abraham's willingness to sacrifice Isaac is about a man who knew that obedience was more important than the tragic loss of his son.

More than any other in the Old Testament, Abraham's story is linked with the promises of God. He leaves his homeland because God promises to give him another. He is amazed when God promises him a son at the age of one hundred, especially since his wife, Sarah, will be ninety when she gives birth! He leads Isaac up a mountain to be sacrificed even though this child is the living embodiment of God's promise. As a result of his faith, he sees the incredible provision of God. As the result of his obedience, Abraham becomes the father, not just of one child or even one nation, but of a multitude of people across time and space, as numerous as the stars in the sky and the grains of sand on the seashore.

Abraham is a great example for you and me. He knew that his relationship with God comes first. When we hear his voice—through his word, a trusted friend, or his whisper in a prayer—we must obey. Nothing else really matters.

Promises in Scripture

I will make your name great,
    and you will be a blessing.
I will bless those who bless you,
    and whoever curses you I will curse.

—Genesis 12:2–3

I will establish my covenant as an everlasting covenant between me and you and your descendants after you for the generations to come, to be your God and the God of your descendants after you.

—Genesis 17:7

Through your offspring all nations on earth will be blessed, because you have obeyed me.

—Genesis 22:18

FRIDAY

HIS LEGACY OF PRAYER

*"Do not be afraid, Abram.
I am your shield,
your very great reward."*

—Genesis 15:1

Reflect On: Genesis 12:10–20.

Praise God: For not hiding his plans but revealing his intentions through the promises he has made.

Offer Thanks: For the way you have benefited from this one man's obedience.

Confess: Your failure at times to believe God's promises.

Ask God: To enable you to make faith visible through your obedience.

The story of Abraham and Isaac on Mount Moriah is one of the most moving in the Bible. But Abraham's story begins well before that, revealing a man who sometimes displayed very little faith. His failures and compromises are key to his story because they show us we are dealing with a human being rather than a cardboard Bible character cutout. His responses convince us that faith grows not in the absence of struggle but right in the middle of it. Like Abraham, we too face setbacks and successes in our life with God. The key to growing more mature in faith is not to focus on our failures but to focus on God's patient, enabling grace.

Lord, you blessed Abraham with land and children and wealth. You used him in ways he could not imagine. But the best promise of all was that you would be his shield and his very great reward. Lord, be my shield too, as well as my very great reward. Amen.

ISAAC

His Name Means *He Laughs*

⟡

His Children:	Esau, Jacob
His Work:	Isaac was an accomplished farmer and herdsman.
His Character:	The only son of Abraham and Sarah, Isaac at a young age witnessed, through the faithfulness of his father, the meaning of obedience. He was gentle and hardworking.
His Sorrow:	As an old and feeble man, Isaac was victimized by the deception of his son Jacob. To his dismay Isaac gave Jacob the blessing he had intended for his older son, Esau.
His Triumph:	Isaac is considered one of the three great patriarchs. For millennia his progeny have revered him.
Key Scriptures:	Genesis 25 – 27

HIS STORY

Isaac always kept an eye on the sky. When there was plenty of rain, his crops flourished. But when there was no rain, there was no harvest. And when there was no harvest, it was time to move on.

The rain had stopped falling. Months passed and the soil turned to dust. Famine settled like a cracked, leathery hide over the gaunt bones of Canaan. Isaac packed up his belongings and moved with his wife to the region of Gerar, a territory of the Philistines, to the place the Lord had sent him.

As a courtesy, Isaac called on King Abimelech to tell the Philistine monarch of his plans and to obtain his consent. "My king, I ask for your permission," Isaac said. "We would like to make a home in the northern portion of this beautiful land."

"You and yours are welcome here," Abimelech greeted him.

Isaac studied the king, wondering at his ready greeting. Was it because he had heard of Isaac's former successes as a farmer? Did he know of Isaac and Isaac's God from the notoriety of his father, Abraham? Or was it because of the beautiful woman who accompanied him?

As Isaac watched, the king's eyes scanned Rebekah from head to toe. "And who is this woman beside you?"

Afraid that someone might kill him to get to her, Isaac tore a page from his father's playbook. "She is my sister," he lied, ignoring her puzzled expression and shielding her from the king and his men.

It didn't take long for the truth to be known, however. One day Abimelech glanced through a window and caught Isaac and Rebekah in a tender embrace.

"She is really your wife!" he said. "Why did you say, 'She is my sister'? What is this you have done to us? One of the men might have slept with your wife, and you would have brought guilt upon us."

With this deception discovered, Abimelech could have thrown Isaac out of his domain. Or worse, he could have executed Isaac for lying to him. But he did neither. Instead, the king issued a decree: "Anyone who molests this man or his wife shall surely be put to death."

Utterly relieved, Isaac went back to work planting crops and raising livestock. Season by season, his success brought him great personal wealth, spreading his borders and outdistancing his neighbors. The king's decision to honor Isaac and keep him in business in the land proved wise.

But Isaac had plenty of detractors. Their jealousy over the king's kindness to Isaac coupled with this outsider's great success—and stunning wife—made these small-minded enemies miserable. And so they filled his wells with dirt, hoping to put him out of business.

Knowing of his people's growing animosity toward Isaac, Abimelech asked Isaac to leave. "Move away from us. You have become too powerful for us."

Thus, in honor of the king's request and for their own safety, Isaac and Rebekah moved to the Valley of Gerar. There Isaac found wells, cisterns that his father had dug and that the

Philistines had also stopped up. But Isaac ran into opposition once more. The locals were not happy to have Isaac settle in their land. "This water is ours," they quarreled. As he reopened the wells, Isaac gave them names signifying the antagonism he faced. One he named "Esek," which meant contention. Another he named "Sitnah," which meant hostility.

Isaac christened another one of these wells "Rehoboth" (meaning "broad places"), saying, "Now the LORD has given us room and we will flourish in the land." Nothing could have more thoroughly summarized Isaac's vision.

After some time had passed, King Abimelech and two of his advisers paid Isaac a visit. He was understandably shocked to see the king and asked, "Why have you come to me, since you were hostile to me and sent me away?"

Their answer may have been as bewildering to Isaac as their surprise visit had been. "We saw clearly that the LORD was with you; so we said, 'There ought to be a sworn agreement between us ... that you will do us no harm, just as we did not molest you but always treated you well and sent you away in peace.'"

Then they added, "And now you are blessed by the LORD."

Isaac called his servants together and ordered them to prepare a feast for Abimelech and his advisers. The evening must have been filled with great celebration, because early the next morning the men swore an oath to each other. Then Isaac sent them on their way, and they left him in peace.

Isaac's heart was filled with gratitude and joy. Even these pagan leaders recognized God's blessing on his life—the result of covenant promises fulfilled.

A LOOK AT THE MAN

A New Address for Success

When a man is hugely successful in his work, everyone notices. Some of those people celebrate his prosperity; others hate him for it. That is what Isaac experienced. He is one of the early farmers in the Scriptures with a remarkable green thumb. "Isaac planted crops in that land and the same year reaped a hundredfold." But Isaac had a secret — something more powerful than a precise crop rotation strategy or specially formulated fertilizer: It was the Lord who was blessing him.

Godly excellence in the marketplace and the generous compensation that often follows it have been subjects of controversy among believers for centuries. Surely Christians are supposed to aspire to serving professions like physicians, missionaries, nurses, and teachers. But is there a place for successful, competitive businesspeople in God's plan as well?

The story of Isaac and Rebekah's years in the land of the Philistines illustrates the answer to these questions — and the reason why. As Isaac and Rebekah were leaving Canaan and looking for a new home, the Lord appeared to Isaac. "Do not go down to Egypt; live in the land where I tell you to live. Stay in this land for a while, and I will be with you and will bless you."

Isaac listened to God's voice and obeyed.

It didn't take long for him to see that his neighbors were envious. The first time Isaac's servant brought word to him that one of his wells had been filled in with dirt would have been a strong indicator! Nothing specific is said about Isaac's reaction to this act of treachery, but there is no indication that Isaac was angry or vengeful. Instead, he simply sent his servants out to re-dig the wells or to find places for new ones.

Next, it was the king's turn to pay Isaac a visit. He asked Isaac to move, sounding much like an Egyptian pharaoh hundreds of years later. Once again Isaac could have been upset at such treatment. "After all I've done for you and your people," Isaac could have said to Abimelech, "this is the way you treat me?"

But he didn't. Instead, Isaac and Rebekah moved on, setting up yet another successful business in a new location.

Then Abimelech paid another visit to Isaac. As he greeted Isaac, the Philistine king summarized why he had come and why he wanted to establish a peace treaty with Isaac. "We saw clearly that the LORD was with you."

Why would a man pursue excellence in business?

The story of Isaac clearly gives us the answer: God had called (and gifted) Isaac for this work, and he was obedient; Isaac had shown respect for those in authority over him; he worked hard, and his efforts were productive; and Isaac did not allow the sabotage of his enemies to discourage or distract him.

What was the result of Isaac's faithfulness? God received the glory, and his name was honored among those who previously did not know or revere him.

HIS LEGACY IN SCRIPTURE

Read Genesis 22:6–12

1. The story of Isaac's near death at the hands of his father is most often considered from Abraham's point of view. But think about Isaac for a moment. What would it have been like to lie on that altar? To escape death by a fraction of a second? To watch as a ram is killed in your place? How do you think this moment shaped the rest of his life?

Read Genesis 26:1–14

2. What similarities do you note between Isaac's experience and his father Abraham's (Genesis 12:10–13) in this passage (vv. 1–6)?

3. Isaac apparently had enough faith to stay in the land of the Philistines but not enough faith to believe God would protect him while he was there (vv. 7–11). Why do you think he wavered? Have you ever experienced similar wavering in your own life? Reflect on what happened during your time of wavering.

4. Why do you think God blessed Isaac even though Isaac lied about Rebekah (vv. 12–14)?

Going Deeper: Read Genesis 21:9–14 and Galatians 4:28–31

5. Isaac was the child of a promise God had made to two people who were long past childbearing age. As Christians, how are we also children of the promise?

HIS LEGACY AS A FATHER

What do your words stand for? When you make a promise to someone, do you mean it? Or do you just move on to the next thing, hoping that if you fail to keep your promise, no one will notice? One of the most powerful lessons to be learned from Isaac as a father is that when a man gives his word, it's a promise.

Isaac had two sons. Esau was the elder and, according to the customs of their day, he was the first in line for his father's blessing—and for the inheritance. Jacob, Isaac's second son, was a cheat. A slick and conniving negotiator. And with his mother's help, Jacob managed to receive Isaac's blessing and the inheritance meant for Esau.

Knowing nothing of this treachery, Esau approached his elderly father a short while later to receive his due. At that moment, Isaac realized he had been deceived and "trembled violently" at the news because he loved Esau more than he loved Jacob. But Isaac had already given his blessing, a once-in-a-lifetime event, to Jacob. Esau wept out loud, something that tough, firstborn sons rarely do. But despite Esau's pleading, Isaac did not recant his promise to Jacob. He had given his word.

Was Isaac angry at Jacob for his deception? Absolutely. Did Isaac wish he could have taken his words back and given the blessing to Esau? Of course. But he refused to compromise.

Isaac was a father who was good for his word. Jesus spoke to the same issue hundreds of years later to a large crowd that must have included many, many fathers. "Let your 'Yes' be 'Yes' and your 'No' 'No'" (Matthew 5:37).

Promises in Scripture

I am the God of your father Abraham. Do not be afraid, for I am with you.

—Genesis 26:24

The LORD blesses his people with peace.

—Psalm 29:11

The blessing of the LORD brings wealth,
and he adds no trouble to it.

—Proverbs 10:22

HIS LEGACY OF PRAYER

Isaac planted crops in that land and the same year reaped a hundredfold, because the LORD blessed him.

—Genesis 26:12

Reflect On: Genesis 25:1 – 31.

Praise God: For his generosity.

Offer Thanks: For the ways God has already blessed you and for all the ways he yet intends to bless you.

Confess: Any tendency to take credit for what God has given you.

Ask God: To richly bless your life as you seek to follow him.

If you look at the divine equation in Isaac's story, it's clear that he received much more than he gave. God required only his obedience, which Isaac gave, though imperfectly. In return, Isaac enjoyed the fulfillment of God's promise in the form of land, children, peace, wealth, and long life. The divine equation still works that way. God gives us everything—shelter, daily provision, his own Son to save us. Only a fool would refuse such an offer.

Father, I thank you for all the ways you have promised to bless your people. Help me to understand these promises and to put my faith in you as the one who is able to bring them to fulfillment. Whatever you ask of me, help me to obey, trusting that you are who you say you are and that you will do what you say you will. Amen.

JACOB

His Name Means *He Grasps the Heel* or *He Deceives*

⟡

His Children: Reuben, Simeon, Levi, Judah, Dan, Naphtali, Gad, Asher, Issachar, Zebulun, Joseph, Benjamin, Dinah.

His Work: As an indentured servant of his Uncle Laban for twenty years (31:38), Jacob was a herdsman.

His Character: With a mother who encouraged it, Jacob learned the art of cunning and deception. In stealing the paternal blessing from his older brother, Jacob was forced to run, experiencing the consequences of his behavior.

His Sorrow: After seven years of hard labor as payment for Rachel, Jacob was deceived by her father, Laban, and was forced to work seven more. During these years he learned firsthand what his own deception had brought on his brother. Later in his life he thought he had lost his son Joseph to an attack by a wild animal.

His Triumph: One of the greatest moments in Jacob's life happened when he was reconciled to his brother, Esau. At the end of his life, he recovered another relationship that appeared to have been lost forever—he discovered that his son Joseph was not only alive, but very successful in Egypt.

Key Scriptures: Genesis 27 – 31

HIS STORY

Jacob hadn't planned this journey. A trip to Haran, over four hundred miles from his home in Canaan, was not something he had ever wanted to undertake—especially as a fugitive. But Jacob was in trouble. The conspiracy between him and his mother to steal the blessing from his older brother had created a deep and painful schism in the family. With Rebekah's encouragement, Jacob had successfully masqueraded as Esau in the presence of his blind father and received the irretrievable blessing.

So awful was the clash between the brothers, Esau made a vow that when their ailing father died, he would kill Jacob. To cool Esau's rage and preserve Jacob's life, Rebekah told Jacob to leave home. His destination was his maternal grandparents' land in Paddan Aram. His objective was twofold: to flee from the peril of his irate brother and to find a wife from among Uncle Laban's daughters.

Endless hours of travel for this lonely man provided ample opportunity for him to review the recent sequence of events and the prospect of living the rest of his life running from his bloodthirsty brother. *This isn't what I had in mind*, Jacob must have thought to himself. *But I have no one to blame but myself.*

The city of Luz, about fifty miles from Beersheba, lay along the road to Haran. When Jacob finally reached it, he found a place to camp for the night. Spreading his blankets and cloak on the ground for a bed, he found a stone just the right size for a pillow and lay down.

But what started out as an ordinary night of slumber from a full day's journey turned into an unforgettable experience. Once asleep, Jacob had a celestial vision he would remember for the rest of his life. In his dream, Jacob saw a stairway. Its first step touched the ground near him and its treads rose into the heavens—like the sloping side of a mighty ziggurat—and Jacob could see angels descending and ascending. His eyes followed the staircase upward until, at the very top, he saw the Lord.

A sighting of the Creator of the universe would have been breathtaking enough, but then the Lord spoke: "I am the LORD, the God of your father Abraham and the God of Isaac. I will give you and your descendants the land on which you are lying.... All peoples on earth will be blessed through you and your offspring. I am with you and will watch over you wherever you go, and I will bring you back to this land. I will not leave you until I have done what I have promised you."

The power of the dream awoke the sleeping Jacob. "Surely the LORD is in this place, and I was not aware of it," Jacob said. Then, as his mind began to embrace the stunning reality of what had happened, he nervously added, "How awesome is this place!"

As sunrise broke the night's hold, Jacob scrambled to his feet, lifted the stone he had used as a pillow, and turned it on its end like a pillar, naming the place Bethel, or "the house of God." As he gazed on his makeshift monument, Jacob made a vow. "If God will be with me and will watch over me on this journey I am taking and will give me food to eat and clothes to wear so that I return safely to my father's house, then the LORD will be my God and this stone that I have set up as a pillar will be God's house, and of all that you give me I will give you a tenth."

Two decades later Jacob had another divine encounter after Jacob's uncle, who became his father-in-law, had given him a strong dose of his own medicine. Laban's multiple deceptions must have reminded Jacob of his own propensity to trickery, especially when Laban promised one daughter in marriage and secretly substituted another. But Jacob stayed there until he secured both sisters as brides, then gathered his family and possessions and slipped away.

Jacob was on the run again. To add to his anxiety, he was about to face his brother, Esau, for the first time since he had fled from Canaan. The day had come for Jacob to face the man whom he had robbed of his father's blessing.

Camped en route to do so, in the middle of a sleepless night, Jacob was startled by the presence of another man. Surprised by the intruder, Jacob wrestled the man to the ground. Strong in both spirit and muscle, Jacob was not overpowered by the man, even though they tussled until dawn. It didn't take long before Jacob realized that his contender was no mere mortal.

When the man realized that he was not going to prevail, he touched Jacob's hip, throwing it out of its socket. Even through the pain, Jacob hung on, grimacing but determined to remain.

"Let me go, for it is daybreak," the man finally said.

But Jacob replied, "I will not let you go unless you bless me."

The man studied him for a moment. "What is your name?"

"Jacob."

"Your name will no longer be Jacob, but Israel, because you have struggled with God and with men and have overcome."

In that moment, his name changed from "Jacob the deceiver" to "Israel the struggler with God," the perfect caption for the rest of his life.

A LOOK AT THE MAN

A Taste of His Own Medicine

Some people's lives seem to glide along with hardly a bump. Like a jockey in parallel cooperation with his horse, they are able to negotiate life's inevitable ups and downs in perfect sequence. No jaw-cracking collisions. No bone-jarring clashes.

And then there are folks like Jacob.

Like a puppy hanging on to someone's pant leg with his teeth, Jacob (meaning "deceiver" or "heel grabber") got dragged and jarred and slammed from one experience to another throughout his life. Of course, he could have let go and lived in relative peace. But that wasn't Jacob.

So what did God do with someone like him? Did he put him in the corner like a naughty child or forever consign him to life's detention hall? No. Instead of putting him away or hiding his adventure-packed story from us, God loved Jacob (Romans 9:13), paid attention to his growth by sending adversaries to challenge him, cared enough to make several personal visits to the man himself, and finally changed his life's course by changing his name.

A great argument that has plagued intellectuals and laypeople alike is this one: Why does God elect some and not others? Why did God, for example, put his sovereign hand on the Jews in the Old Testament to the obvious exclusion of other peoples? Libraries are filled with volumes dealing with this worrisome question.

However, the real question should not be why God seems to overlook some but, considering our sinfulness and mutinous desires, why does God choose to favor anyone at all?

As we look back at Jacob's life, we see a man whom God loved with a special kind of affection. God saw Jacob as a paradigm of his people, capable of equal amounts of rebellion and repentance, disobedience and confession.

One of the confirmations of God's peculiar love for Jacob was his adversity-filled life. The conflicts within his family were obvious. Forever the younger brother, Jacob must have been slighted by his father's favoritism of his older brother. He may have felt manipulated by his mother's schemes as she used him to fulfill her own plans. He lived with frustration in the house of Laban. And he knew the relentless dread of living as a fugitive. In all of these, Jacob was culpable, but God was preparing him for greatness.

For believers, God's presence through the person of the Holy Spirit is constant. But there are only a handful of times when Scripture records a face-to-face encounter between God and people. In his first dream, Jacob sees God standing at the pinnacle of the stairway to heaven. "I am with you and will watch over you wherever you go," the Lord said to Jacob. Twenty years later God meets Jacob in the form of a man. As a perfect template of Jacob's spiritual journey, Jacob grapples with a man sent from the Lord. And then, just before the man leaves the crippled Jacob, he gives him a new name and blesses him when he asks for it. At last Jacob learns that the blessing that counts comes from the Father of all.

You may know someone just like Jacob. You may *be* someone like Jacob. God loves you. Adversity is his gift to you. His presence through his Spirit is real. And he has given you a new name. You're a Christian.

HIS LEGACY IN SCRIPTURE

Read Genesis 25:22–26

1. Like Isaac's mother Sarah, Isaac's wife, Rebekah, seemed incapable of bearing children. The two had been married twenty years before she finally gave birth to twins, Esau and Jacob. It was almost as if God were setting up obstacles to the fulfillment of his own promise. Why do you think God allowed things to unfold in this way?

2. God made an unconventional choice, choosing the younger son over the firstborn. What does this say about the surprising way God chooses to fulfill his promises?

Read Genesis 27:1–13, 27–35

3. What does this plot between mother and son reveal about their character? Did God need this kind of help to ensure that the promised blessing would be passed on through Jacob and not Esau? Why or why not?

4. What kind of family dynamic was at work in Jacob's home that allowed him to steal the blessing from his older brother? What does this say about God's ability to achieve his purposes despite human weakness and sin?

Read Genesis 29:16–27

5. Soon after deceiving his father and robbing his brother of his blessing, Jacob fled for his life to Paddan Aram, the home of his Uncle Laban. Seven years later Jacob became the deceived rather than the deceiver, tricked by Laban into marrying his older daughter. Does this story have implications regarding how our actions toward others may come back to haunt us? If so, how?

Going Deeper: Read Genesis 32:22–31

6. This scene takes place twenty years after Jacob fled his home to escape his brother's wrath. By now his life has been marked by a series of struggles. In this passage we see him struggling, not with mere human beings but with God, insisting, "I will not let you go unless you bless me." Why do you think Jacob received the new name Israel? What is the significance of the limp he incurred during this supernatural wrestling match? Have you ever felt that you have been engaged in some kind of struggle with God? If so, how?

HIS LEGACY AS A FATHER

As a father, you know that treating your children equally can be a major challenge. In his later years, Jacob (Israel) gives us a strong reminder of what happens when a dad doesn't deal evenly with his family.

Joseph, Jacob's eleventh son, must have made his aged father very proud. He worked hard in the fields and brought Jacob the inside scoop on the rest of his family. Jacob allowed young Joseph to become his personal confidant and emissary and openly rewarded him for the special place he had found in his father's heart.

Joseph's brothers reacted predictably. Their father's foolish indiscretion predictably forced them to hate their little brother.

Treating each of our children with an equal amount of love, attention, and discipline will foster the best possible relationship they could ever have with each other. Affectionately singling one of your children out—perhaps the one who, by some quirk of genetic fate, will become the scholar or the athlete you never were—could very well sentence your children to rivalry and bitterness.

Our children must experience the full measure of their father's love. If they don't, they may find a way to get your attention ... such as selling "Dad's favorite" to total strangers.

Promises in Scripture

May God give you of heaven's dew
*   and of earth's richness—*
an abundance of grain and new wine.

—Genesis 27:28

I am with you and will watch over you wherever you go,
and I will bring you back to this land. I will not leave
you until I have done what I have promised you.

—Genesis 28:15

This is what the Sovereign LORD, the Holy One of
*   Israel, says:*
"In repentance and rest is your salvation,
*   in quietness and trust is your strength."*

—Isaiah 30:15

HIS LEGACY OF PRAYER

When Jacob awoke from his sleep, he thought, "Surely the LORD is in this place, and I was not aware of it.... This is none other than the house of God; this is the gate of heaven."

—Genesis 28:16–17

Reflect On: Genesis 28:10–22.

Praise God: For being with you even when you didn't know it.

Offer Thanks: For God's determination to keep his promises.

Confess: Any tendency to "help" God by using the wrong means.

Ask God: To give you greater confidence in his ability to provide for you as well as for those in your care.

One of the most famous dreams ever recorded is the one Jacob had when he fled from his brother. Alone in the wilderness, using a stone for a pillow, he dreamed of a stairway connecting earth and heaven. In his dream he saw angels moving up and down. He awoke with a sense of awe, pledging to give back to God a tenth of everything God would give him in the future. For a moment, Jacob was no longer scheming and striving to get ahead. Instead, he was simply responding with worship, thanksgiving, and trust to the God who promised to care for him.

Lord, help me to sense your presence in my life and to rest in the confidence that you can take care of me far better than I can take care of myself. Thank you for everything you've given me. Please give me the faith to set aside some of these blessings so that I can give them back to you. Amen.

AARON

His Work: Aaron was the first in the line of Israel's hereditary priesthood.

His Children: Nadab, Abihu, Eleazar, and Ithamar

His Character: Aaron's role was primarily a passive one: to do and say whatever Moses told him to. Though he stood by Moses throughout his struggle with Pharaoh, he seemed unable to stand on his own as a leader. When Moses was absent for forty days, Aaron gave in to the people's insistent demands for a god to worship. On another occasion, however, he joined Moses in stopping a plague that threatened to destroy the Israelites because of their rebellion.

His Sorrow: Aaron disobeyed the Lord by presiding over an incident of false worship. At another point he angered God by joining his sister Miriam in complaining against their brother's leadership.

His Triumph: To have spoken God's word, entrusted to him through Moses, and eventually to have acted as a mediator between God and man, providing for the atonement of sin and the people's reconciliation with God.

Key Scriptures: Exodus 20:1–6; 28; 32; Numbers 12:1–15

HIS STORY

Aaron was as perplexed as anyone by his brother Moses' long absence from the camp. Moses and his aide Joshua had been on the mountain forty days and forty nights. Had Moses been eaten by wild animals? Had he fallen off a cliff? Had he been consumed by the fire that covered the top of Mount Sinai?

Growing impatient and fearful, the Israelites in the valley below gathered around Aaron and demanded, "Come, make us gods who will go before us. As for this fellow Moses who brought us up out of Egypt, we don't know what has happened to him." Aaron opened his mouth to reply, but nothing came out. What could he say? Moses had always supplied the words, straight from the mouth of God. But for more than a month there had been no words, and the people had grown restless, in need of assurance of the divine presence, fearful they would perish without a god to guide them on their wilderness journey.

Aaron had to act. The people were demanding it. So he told the Israelites, "Take off the gold earrings that your wives, your sons, and your daughters are wearing, and bring them to me." Then he took the gold and made it into an idol cast in the shape of a calf, hoping that the bull would remind the people of God's power and strength.

But as soon as the calf emerged gleaming and golden from the fire, the leaders cried out, "These are your gods, O Israel, who brought you up out of Egypt." Attempting to redirect their worship, Aaron built an altar in front of the calf and announced, "Tomorrow there will be a festival to the LORD." So the next day the people got up early and sacrificed burnt offerings. But as the day wore on, they began to worship the calf in an orgy of drunkenness, behaving more like pagans than those who worshiped the Lord.

Meanwhile, on the mountain called Sinai, Moses had enjoyed forty days and nights in the presence of God, where the Lord had entrusted him with detailed instructions for shaping the life of his people. The first two of the ten commandments God had inscribed on two stone tablets were these:

> *You shall have no other gods before me.*
> *You shall not make for yourself an idol in the form of anything in heaven above or on the earth beneath or in the waters below. You shall not bow down to them or worship them; for I, the LORD your God, am a jealous God, punishing the children for the sin of the fathers to the third and fourth generation of those who hate me, but showing love to a thousand generations of those who love me and keep my commandments.*

Day after day, Moses talked with God. On the fortieth day, he heard God's voice, and this time there was anger in it: "Go down, because your people, whom you brought up out of Egypt, have become corrupt. They are a stiff-necked people. Now leave me alone so that my anger may burn against them and that I may destroy them. Then I will make you into a great nation."

But Moses pleaded with God, reminding him of his covenant: "O LORD, why should your anger burn against your people, whom you brought out of Egypt with great power and a mighty hand? Why should the Egyptians say, 'It was with evil intent that he brought them out, to kill them in the mountains and to wipe them off the face of the earth'? Turn from your fierce anger; relent and do not bring disaster on your people."

The Lord graciously relented, and Moses made his way down the mountain carrying the two tablets containing the writing of God.

When Aaron saw Moses coming, he felt relieved and yet afraid of what might happen next. As soon as Moses saw the calf and the dancing, he threw the tablets down on the ground, breaking them to pieces at the foot of the mountain. Then he took the calf and burned it in the fire and ground it to powder. He scattered the powder in water and made the people drink it.

Then he turned his attention toward Aaron: "What did these people do to you, that you led them into such great sin?"

Aaron tried to excuse himself: "Do not be angry, my lord. You know how prone these people are to evil. When you didn't come back, they demanded an image to worship."

To Moses, it sounded like the oldest of excuses, like the one Adam had used to excuse himself for his disobedience in Eden, saying to God: "The woman you put here with me—she gave me some fruit from the tree, and I ate it."

That day Moses ordered the Levites to kill those who had been unfaithful. Three thousand people perished as a result. Then Moses spoke to God on behalf of all the people, saying, "Oh, what a great sin these people have committed! They have made themselves gods of gold. But now, please forgive their sin — but if not, then blot me out of the book you have written."

But God refused to punish Moses and said instead, "Whoever has sinned against me I will blot out of my book. Now go, lead the people to the place I spoke of, and my angel will go before you."

After so great a betrayal, God led Moses and Aaron and all the people through the desert, still promising to be their God, still promising he would lead them to a land flowing with milk and honey. And all the days of his life Aaron remained a priest of God.

A LOOK AT THE MAN

An Imperfect Intercessor

After the incident with the calf, Aaron must have been aware of the seriousness of his failure to lead the people and of his own need for forgiveness. He would have realized that his life had been in jeopardy because of God's anger. But Aaron was spared because of God's merciful response to his brother's prayers.

Aaron was a man who had witnessed God's power over Pharaoh and who had for a time stood on the mountain with Moses and seen the glory of God. As one who was set apart by God to play an important role among his people, he had a unique part to play in the story of salvation. And yet even his kinship with Moses, even God's call to be a priest, did not spare him from the power of sin's temptation.

Thereafter, whenever Aaron performed his priestly duties as a mediator between a holy God and a sinful people, he would not be able to come before the Lord with any air of self-righteousness, as though only the people, and not he, were guilty of sin. Because of his own weakness, he would be capable of sympathizing with the weakness of God's people.

A priest's ability to sympathize with the people, as it turns out, was only half of what God had planned. Centuries later there would be a man who would perfectly embody the role of the high priest, not only sympathizing with the weakness of his people, but also resisting the power of temptation. Because of him, we are now able to approach God, confident that his attitude toward each of us is marked by grace and mercy (see Hebrews 4:14 – 16).

HIS LEGACY IN SCRIPTURE

Read Exodus 28:29–30, 36–38

1. In these passages, the Lord instructed Moses how the priestly garments should be designed. What did these garments signify about Aaron's role as a priest?

Read Exodus 32:1–14

2. What do Aaron's actions say about his character? About his leadership?

3. The Israelites had already seen incredible evidence of God's power—the ten plagues in Egypt, the parting of the Red Sea, the miraculous provision of manna in the desert. Why do you think they were still tempted by idol worship?

4. Why do you think God calls the Israelites "your" people in verse 7?

5. Moses interceded for Aaron and the people in specific ways in verses 11–13. Comment on the nature and effectiveness of his prayer.

Going Deeper: Read Numbers 12:1–15

6. Moses, Aaron, and Miriam were all prophets through whom God had spoken. Yet Aaron and Miriam chafed under the leadership of their younger brother. What does this story say about sin's power to invade the

community of God's people regardless of how powerfully God has been at work in their midst?

7. In his role as priest, Aaron was a mediator between God and the people, making sacrifices before a holy God to deal with the people's sin and weakness. Imperfect as he was, his priesthood foreshadowed the perfect high priesthood of Jesus. The book of Hebrews makes this plain:

> *Therefore, since we have a great high priest who has gone through the heavens, Jesus the Son of God, let us hold firmly to the faith we profess. For we do not have a high priest who is unable to sympathize with our weaknesses, but we have one who has been tempted in every way, just as we are — yet was without sin. Let us then approach the throne of grace with confidence, so that we may receive mercy and find grace to help us in our time of need. (Hebrews 4:14 – 16)*

Why is it important to have a high priest who can both sympathize with our weakness and resist sin?

HIS LEGACY AS A FATHER

As it turns out, Aaron's leadership problems weren't confined to his priestly failures in his responsibilities over the Israelites. These problems included some serious trouble at home.

Aaron had four sons, and each of these men followed in their dad's footsteps as priests.

Nadab and Abihu, Aaron's older sons, were about to offer a sacrifice to God. Although the Bible doesn't give all the details, it does say that their sacrifice was "unauthorized." It doesn't matter whether these men were defiant in this illegal act or just sloppy about what they were doing. Either way the result was lethal. "So fire came out from the presence of the LORD and consumed them, and they died before the LORD" (Leviticus 10:2).

Of course, these were grown men. Regardless of the bad example their father, Aaron, had set in the wilderness years before, they *had* the capacity to make a good decision before the Lord. But the pattern they followed was just like their dad, their foolish spontaneity reminiscent of the awful episode with the golden calf.

Grown children are responsible before God for their actions. No excuses will do. But the example that their fathers set for them can put them on a course that models faithfulness, obedience, fidelity, and discipline—or something else.

Promises in Scripture

If God is for us, who can be against us? He who did not spare his own Son, but gave him up for us all—how will he not also, along with him, graciously give us all things?

—Romans 8:31–32

I will put my laws in their hearts,
and I will write them on their minds. . . .
Their sins and lawless acts
I will remember no more.

—Hebrews 10:16–17

If we walk in the light, as he is in the light, we have fellowship with one another, and the blood of Jesus, his Son, purifies us from all sin.

—1 John 1:7

HIS LEGACY OF PRAYER

So Aaron did as Moses said, and ran into the midst of the assembly. The plague had already started among the people, but Aaron offered the incense and made atonement for them. He stood between the living and the dead, and the plague stopped.

—Numbers 16:47–48

Reflect On: Hebrews 4:14–16.

Praise God: For providing us with a great high priest.

Offer Thanks: That God has made a way for us to return to him.

Confess: Any pride that makes you want to live life strictly on your own terms.

Ask God: To increase your confidence in his forgiveness.

God himself had called the Israelites a "stiff-necked people" because they were constantly complaining, questioning, resisting, and rebelling. On one occasion when the people were ready to mount a revolt and return to Egypt, Aaron stepped into the midst of them and stopped a plague that broke out as a result of God's judgment. Sin always carries its own set of plagues in the form of broken relationships and wasted lives. But Christ is ready to stand between the living and the dead, able to halt sin's deadly effects so that we can live in the presence of God.

Father, you already know how stiff-necked I can sometimes be. Don't let me get away with being stubborn toward you even in the smallest things. Help me come to the throne of grace, confident that I will receive the help I need. In Jesus' name, Amen.

ACHAN

His Name Means *Troublemaker*

⬥

His Children:	Unnamed sons and daughters (Joshua 7:24)
His Character:	Achan's greed for the spoils of war and his attempt to hide his sin led to a situation that endangered Israel's relationship with God. By disregarding God's command, he brought trouble and judgment on his own people.
His Sorrow:	His disobedience resulted in the loss of many lives, including his own.
His Triumph:	To have participated in the victory over Jericho.
Key Scriptures:	Joshua 7:1 – 8:2

HIS STORY

It was daybreak of the seventh day. During the past six days, Jericho had been under siege. But there were no battering rams, ladders, or axes. Nor were there chariots or well-armed soldiers ready to rush into the city as soon as the walls were breached. There were only men marching, day after day, in silent procession around the walls, trumpets blaring as they encircled the city. Each man held his tongue, exactly as Joshua had instructed: "Do not give a war cry, do not raise your voices, do not say a word until the day I tell you to shout. Then shout!"

At first there were catcalls from the men standing sentry on the walls, but after six days the siege had created a sense of dread among Jericho's inhabitants, so strong that it silenced even these. How long would the Israelites keep marching? Were they planning to take the city by magic or by trickery? When would they strike? The incessant blare of trumpets grated on their nerves and made them edgy.

As the sun rose over Jericho, Achan, of Judah's tribe, joined the rest of Israel's army, falling in line behind the priests, who marched before the ark. This time the soldiers proceeded around the city, not once but seven times, and Achan looked up at faces that had now grown familiar — Jericho's guards standing duty on the city walls. "All of them," he thought, "will be dead by sunset."

Earlier, Joshua had instructed the Israelites, telling them, "The city and all that is in it are to be devoted to the LORD. [Everyone and everything was to be destroyed.] Only Rahab the prostitute [a woman who had protected Israel's spies] and all who are with her in her house shall be spared.... But keep away from the devoted things, so that you will not bring about your own destruction by taking any of them. Otherwise you will make the camp of Israel liable to destruction and bring trouble on it. All the silver and gold and the articles of bronze and iron are sacred to the LORD and must go into his treasury."

Suddenly Achan heard the sound of a trumpet blast followed by Joshua's urgent command: "Shout! For the LORD has given you the city!" A loud cry went up from all the people, and the walls of Jericho crumbled like day-old bread crushed between a man's fingers. Along with all the other Israelites, Achan rushed into the city, slaughtering the enemies of Israel and sparing no one. Even the animals were put to the sword.

After a time, once the chaos had diminished, Achan found himself alone in a house. Stepping over the dead bodies, he saw something that caught him fast and held him — spoils from the new land — a beautiful robe draped across a chair, a mound of silver, a wedge of gold. Perhaps the people who lived here had meant to escape with their treasures. He remembered Joshua's warning that the spoils belonged to the Lord. Any man who acted otherwise would bring trouble on Israel. But what trouble could come from merely touching the robe and feeling the heft of the silver and the gold? Surely the garment was the finest he had ever seen.

Did God really intend that something as marvelous as this robe was to be destroyed? Hadn't he promised to give the land to his people, a land flowing with milk and honey? Why, thought Achan, *should I deprive my family of the good things my own hands have won?* He rubbed the robe against his skin, caressing it as though it were a lover he could not part with. Then he wrapped the gold and silver carefully inside the robe's folds, tucking the precious package beneath his tunic and fleeing the house just in time to see men running through the city setting fires.

After Jericho's defeat, Joshua sent three thousand men to Ai, a town fifteen miles to the west. But though his army should have scored an easy victory, they were defeated and thirty-six men were killed. Stunned by this sudden reversal in battle, Joshua fell on his face before the ark of the Lord, crying out: "Sovereign LORD, why did you ever bring this people across the Jordan to deliver us into the hands of the Amorites to destroy us? What can I say, now that Israel has been routed? The Canaanites and the other people of the country will hear about this and they will surround us and wipe out our name from the earth. What then will you do for your own great name?"

"Stand up!" the Lord commanded. "What are you doing down on your face? Israel has sinned; they have violated my covenant, which I commanded them to keep. That is why the Israelites cannot stand against their enemies. I will not be with you anymore unless you destroy whatever among you is devoted to destruction."

So Joshua ordered the Israelites to assemble early the next morning, and Achan stood with other men from the tribe of

Judah. As the sun passed behind a cloud, Achan shivered, folding his arms across his chest as if to defend himself against advancing shadows. One by one, lots were cast to determine who had violated God's command. First the tribe of Judah was taken. Then the clan of the Zerahites. Then the family of Zimri — Achan's own family. He wanted to run but couldn't, as though stuck in a dream he could not escape. Man by man, each member of the family was called forward until, finally, inevitably, the lot fell to Achan, the son of Carmi, the son of Zimri, the son of Zerah, of the tribe of Judah.

"It is true," Achan confessed, words rushing from his mouth. "I have sinned against the LORD, the God of Israel. This is what I have done: When I saw in the plunder a beautiful robe from Babylonia, two hundred shekels of silver and a wedge of gold weighing fifty shekels, I coveted them and took them. They are hidden in the ground inside my tent, with the silver underneath."

Then Joshua, together with all Israel, took Achan; the silver; the robe; the gold wedge; his sons and daughters; his cattle, donkeys, and sheep; his tent and all that he had to the valley of Achor. And Joshua said, "Why have you brought this trouble on us? The LORD will bring trouble on you today."

Then the people of Israel stoned him, and after they had stoned his family, they burned them. Over Achan they heaped a large pile of rocks, which remained for many years. Then Joshua sent a force of thirty thousand fighting men to attack Ai, and God delivered the city into their hands.

A LOOK AT THE MAN

No Place to Hide

Achan may not have been a bad man, at least to begin with. While living for many years in the desert, he may even have fed himself on dreams of what life would be like in the Promised Land, where he could build a life for his family. He may have rushed into Jericho fully intending to follow the Lord's commands. But then came an opportunity to do otherwise. And that's when his resolve faded.

Achan's disobedience then produced a kind of foolishness in him: He attempted to hide what he had done, burying stolen goods beneath his tent. But he was hiding from the God who made him, from the same God who parted the Red Sea and the Jordan River, and from the God who had just caused the walls of a fortified city to crumble without a weapon being raised against it. Why was Achan foolish enough to think that God would have a tough time seeing through his little deception?

It's sin's nature to hide. Consider your own experience. Isn't it hard to admit your sins to others? And isn't it even difficult to admit them to yourself? Most of us have found ingenious ways to hide the ugliness of sin from ourselves and others by rationalizing, excusing, and even forgetting things we've done wrong. But Achan's story tells us that God is never fooled by such foolishness.

Simple obedience and the cleansing power of God's grace are the best defense against sin. But when we fail to do the right thing, we should remind ourselves not to compound the problem by hiding what we've done. Instead, we can go directly to God, expressing our sorrow and asking his forgiveness, confident that he will give it.

HIS LEGACY IN SCRIPTURE

Read Joshua 6:16–21

1. This practice of "devoting" everything in the city to destruction seems harsh to us. Moses advocated this approach, pointing out that otherwise the native peoples of the Promised Land would lead the Israelites into idol worship and other forms of corruption (Deuteronomy 16–18). Still, we must be careful to understand the context of this ancient story, which unfolded in a specific time and place. To use such a story to rationalize the unjust treatment of individuals or entire groups of people today would be to misread Scripture with terrible consequences. How then are we to apply the story? It might help to consider whether there is a spiritual parallel in your own life. What things need to be utterly destroyed before you can follow God wholeheartedly?

Read Joshua 7:1–25

2. Why do you think verse 1 describes Achan in terms of his tribal relationships? Achan's sin highlights the truth that there is no such thing as private morality. How have you seen sin affect an entire community?

3. The ancient Israelites operated under different notions of justice than we do. In Achan's case, his entire family was destroyed for his sin. Read Ezekiel

18:1–4, 14–24 and comment on how God's unfolding revelation in Ezekiel helped the Israelites understand how God intends to deal with individual sin and righteousness.

4. Israel's defeat at the hand of a much smaller force of enemies points to the spreading effects of sin among the community of God's people. Why do you think Achan's sin affected everyone else? How do our own sins affect the community of believers?

5. Achan describes his temptation in detail—"a beautiful robe from Babylonia," "a wedge of gold weighing fifty shekels." We can almost imagine him fingering the robe as he marveled over its workmanship. What a pity, he must have thought, to destroy such a beautiful garment. At that moment, Achan succumbed to sin's central temptation: to do what he thought was right rather than what God said was right. How can you guard against the temptation to base your actions on your own judgment rather than on God's?

Going Deeper: Read Joshua 7:25–26

6. How does this memorial made of stones differ from the first memorial the Israelites made after crossing over the Jordan River (see Joshua 4:4–7)? What was God trying to convey to his people as they began their conquest of Canaan?

HIS LEGACY AS A FATHER

The account of Achan's disobedience is one of the most graphic in the entire Bible. It's so vicious and violent that many teachers have found themselves tempted to skip over it rather than to invite predictable questions about God's unthinkable harshness. Achan strikes a tragic silhouette against the backdrop of God's chosen people. But imagine what it must have been like to be one of his children.

No doubt, the sons and daughters of Achan had heard about the surprising defeat of the Israelites at Ai. Thirty-six men had been killed in a battle that should have taken no one at all. And now Joshua was frightened. He ordered an impromptu assembly of all the men of Israel. Thousands stood ready while lots were drawn, culling the innocent from the one guilty man who dared defy the unqualified command of the Lord God.

Achan's children's pulses must have quickened as the lots narrowed down to their father. One painful lot after another, the spotlight found its way to their dad. They watched in horror as Achan — the man they loved and trusted — slumped to the ground at Joshua's feet, pleading in vain for mercy.

We can only imagine how Achan felt as he approached his waiting family. His mission was not only to tell them that Joshua had pronounced a death sentence on *his* disobedience, but that each member of his family and even their animals would soon be pummeled and crushed, their corpses buried under a pile of rocks.

When a father chooses to disobey God's clearly prescribed laws, his commands and precepts, it is not only his own heart that suffers the consequences. His children, too, often stand in line to bear the scars as sinful patterns and habits are reproduced from one generation to the next.

Promises in Scripture

> *Do not be wise in your own eyes;*
> *fear the LORD and shun evil.*
> *This will bring health to your body*
> *and nourishment to your bones.*

—Proverbs 3:7–8

> *This is what the LORD says:*
> *"Stand at the crossroads and look …*
> *ask where the good way is, and walk in it,*
> *and you will find rest for your souls."*

—Jeremiah 6:16

> *But if you do warn the righteous man not to sin and he does not sin, he will surely live because he took warning, and you will have saved yourself.*

—Ezekiel 3:21

HIS LEGACY OF PRAYER

"Oh, that their hearts would be inclined to fear me and keep all my commands always, so that it might go well with them and their children forever!"

— Deuteronomy 5:29

Reflect On: Deuteronomy 6:1 – 3.

Praise God: Because his commandments are meant to bless us, not to enslave us.

Offer Thanks: That God has not hidden his commands from us.

Confess: Any tendency to value your opinion about a course of action more than you value God's.

Ask God: To make you humble enough to realize that you do not always know what is best.

Fear is a healthy thing if it keeps a young child from crossing a busy street by himself or from toying with an angry dog. Similarly, fearing God, as a child might fear his parents, is a healthy part of the Christian life because it keeps us from dangers we often cannot see or understand. Achan's story drives home the consequences of a man's failure to fear God enough to keep a commandment he did not fully understand. His life needs to remind us of the good things we will certainly forfeit if we live in a way that shows our disregard for God's law.

Father, I want to obey your commandments—all of them. But I know from past experience that I can't just grit my teeth and leave it at that. The only way I can do what you ask me to do is by relying on your Holy Spirit to work inside me, strengthen me, and change my heart. Lord, help me to fear you, love your Word, and act in a way that honors you. In your name, Amen.

DAVID

His Name May Mean *Beloved*

⌒◯◯⌒

His Children: Amnon, Daniel, Absalom, Adonijah, Shephatiah, Ithream, Shammua, Shobab, Nathan, Solomon, Ibhar, Elishua, Eliphelet, Nogah, Nepheg, Japhia, Elishama, Eliada, Eliphelet, and Tamar

His Work: A shepherd by trade, David became the second king of Israel.

His Character: A man of stark contrasts, David was a man who did nothing halfheartedly. Though he sinned terribly, his repentance was deep and lasting. Scripture refers to him as "a man after God's own heart."

His Sorrow: During his lifetime, David had to come to grips with his own sinfulness and the severity of God's punishment, such as the death of his sons and his inability to build the temple.

His Triumph: Under David's leadership, the nation of Israel reached prominence as it had never known before.

Key Scripture: 1 Samuel 17

HIS STORY

"David."

Jesse's voice echoed off the hillsides until it reached the ears of a shepherd boy watching over his flock in a meadow outside Bethlehem.

"David!"

The young man gathered his things and ran home to meet his father, Jesse, who had an assignment for him. "Take this sack of roasted grain and these ten loaves of bread for your brothers and hurry to their camp. Take along these ten cheeses to the commander of their unit. See how your brothers are and bring back some assurance from them. They are with Saul and all the men of Israel in the valley of Elah, fighting against the Philistines."

The young shepherd eagerly agreed. The battlefront sounded far more exciting than the pasture anyway. So David made arrangements for the care of his sheep and set out to meet his brothers. Though the journey to the front lasted only a single morning, it changed the course of David's life.

He reached camp just as the army was marching to its battle position. Eager to watch his older brothers in action, David ran to the front line. To his surprise, instead of an army of Philistines, he found that the Israelites faced only one man and his shield bearer, standing defiantly before them in the open field. That one man, however, stood over nine feet tall, and his armor weighed as much as a small man. Like a schoolyard bully, the giant drew a line in the sand, challenging the Israelites.

"Choose a man and have him come down to me," he shouted. "If he is able to fight and kill me, we will become your subjects; but if I overcome him and kill him, you will become our subjects and serve us. This day I defy the ranks of Israel! Give me a man, and let us fight each other."

For forty consecutive days, Goliath's words had bellowed throughout the valley of Elah and straight into the hearts and faltering knees of the terrified Israelite army. Even Saul, their mighty leader, was afraid.

Winding his way through the ranks of soldiers, David pestered anyone who would pay attention to him, "What will be done for the man who kills this Philistine and removes this disgrace from Israel?"

Seasoned infantrymen looked down to see who was asking this presumptuous question. If it hadn't come from a mere boy, they would have been offended by the insinuation. As it was, they chortled at his naivety.

Standing in the crowd of soldiers was Eliab, David's oldest brother. *Who is that?* he asked himself. *His voice sounds familiar.* Turning around, he was enraged to see his little brother David. "Why have you come down here?" he barked. "And with whom did you leave those few sheep in the desert?" The older brother's jealousy burst from his lips. "I know how conceited you are and how wicked your heart is. You came down only to watch the battle."

"Now what have I done?" David replied. "Can't I even speak?"

Soon Saul, the king of Israel, heard that there was a youngster in the camp stirring up the ire of his men. "Go get him," Saul ordered one of his lieutenants.

David's first words as he stepped into the presence of the commander in chief of the armies of Israel—a place few soldiers had the right to stand—were these: "Let no one lose heart on account of this Philistine; your servant will go and fight him."

"You are not able to go out against this Philistine and fight him," Saul replied, his heart filled with a mixture of indignation and pity. "Goliath has been a fighting man since his youth."

That was all the boy needed to hear. "I've been a fighting man since my youth, too," David said, as he confidently summarized his experience for the king. "Your servant has killed both the lion and the bear; this uncircumcised Philistine will be like one of them, because he has defied the armies of the living God. The LORD who delivered me from the paw of the lion and the paw of the bear will deliver me from the hand of this Philistine."

Saul had never seen courage like this. *If only my soldiers could say the same*, Saul must have thought. *If only I had this boy's faith*, he might have added.

Moments later a boy holding only a sling and five smooth stones stood before a fully armed giant holding a spear, the point of which weighed fifteen pounds. "Am I a dog?" Goliath shouted. "Come here, and I'll give your flesh to the birds of the air and the beasts of the field."

"You come against me with sword and spear and javelin, but I come against you in the name of the LORD Almighty, the God of the armies of Israel, whom you have defied," cried David.

An instant later the giant was nothing but a headless carcass, his warm blood soaking into the dry sand of the Valley of Elah.

According to the bargain he had offered, Goliath's defeat was supposed to transform the Philistine soldiers into servants of the Israelites. But in spite of the rules of the game, they fled for their lives like frightened schoolboys. Coming face to face not with a giant but with an eager emissary of the living God had scared the Philistines to death and altered the balance of power between the two nations.

A LOOK AT THE MAN

The Boy Who Would Be King

It's the stuff of epic cinematography—hillsides filled with thousands of jostling soldiers, clattering armaments, and everything at stake. But the heart of the story of David and Goliath is real. It's the story of a young man who threw himself at life with great abandonment, confident as he was in the goodness and power of the God of Abraham, Isaac, and Jacob.

There were two defining moments in David's childhood. The first happened when Samuel visited his father's home looking for the man who would someday be king. The youngest son and least likely candidate, David, came in from the pasture to receive the prophet's anointing and then went back to work.

The second defining moment came when he encountered Goliath in a contest that would determine the outcome of a battle. Forerunners of the ancient Greeks, the Philistines were accustomed to deciding battles in an arena rather than between armies. In addition to saving lives, such contests indulged the desire to turn warfare into sport. Centuries later Rome picked up the same idea. The Philistine army must have thought they had it made with a warrior like Goliath in their ranks. But they didn't reckon on the young boy who believed that God was capable of anything. Winding his way through the company of Israel's soldiers, David's innocent questions were met with shock and derision. But David was astounded by the Israelites' lack of faith.

Even the king was afraid. "Don't you know who you're fighting for?" David asked Saul. "Where's your trust in him?"

The courage David exhibited as a young man who defended his father's sheep from wild animals and then defended God's people from a godless thug lasted throughout his life. And the same confidence in the God of his fathers marked his life in the years that followed.

Though David wasn't a perfect man, he confessed his sins with the same unfettered confidence in God that had marked his previous dealings. And because he never blamed anyone but himself when he fell, he received God's mercy with no impediments.

Almost five hundred years later the prophet Isaiah would write:

> Seek the LORD while he may be found;
>   call on him while he is near.
> Let the wicked forsake his way
>   and the evil man his thoughts.
> Let him turn to the Lord, and he will have mercy on
>   him,
>   and to our God, for he will freely pardon.
>
> Isaiah 55:6–7

Perhaps Isaiah was remembering David, the man whose courage, confidence, faith, contrition, and trust in God's mercy knew no limits.

David lived without restraint. No giant would deter him. He took the promises of the living God for his own and seized life with the certainty of knowing that God was with him. This was the legacy of the "man after God's own heart."

HIS LEGACY IN SCRIPTURE

Read 1 Samuel 17:1–50

1. What does the scene in verses 1–11 indicate about the condition of Israel and Saul's faith in the covenant promises of God?

2. As astonishing as David's courage was, it is also astonishing that Saul put him forth as Israel's champion, since the boy's defeat would have meant the defeat of the entire Israelite force. Why do you think he took the risk?

3. Goliath, the giant who looked so impossible to defeat, was quickly dispatched by a boy armed with nothing but a sling, a stone, and unwavering faith, which must have seemed like foolishness to many. When have you needed this kind of faith to defeat an overwhelming obstacle? Describe the circumstances.

Going Deeper: Read 1 Samuel 24:1–15

4. Saul became so jealous of David that David fled to the wilderness for fear of his life. What does this passage tell you about David's character?

5. David was Israel's greatest king. Of course, the prophecies in the Hebrew Scriptures concerning his eternal kingdom were not fulfilled in his lifetime. Instead, they were reserved for the man the Gospels often refer to as the "Son of David"—Jesus Christ. Psalm 22 is

one of the many psalms attributed to David. Read it through once and think about how it expresses the story of David, particularly during the period when he was fleeing from Saul. Now read it again in light of what you know about the story of Jesus.

HIS LEGACY AS A FATHER

David's résumé was filled with great accomplishments. Killing lions and bears to protect his father's sheep and felling a giant with a single stone were just a few of them. But David's performance as a father was marred by tragedy.

Absalom was David's fourth son (Solomon was his tenth). In many ways, Absalom was as gifted as his father. He was a great strategist and a natural-born leader, and he had a winsome way with people. But Absalom hated his father and was leading a rebellion against him. David was unwilling to confront his boy. This unwillingness perilously divided the kingdom. Many followed Absalom; others remained loyal to David.

Of course, David was vulnerable because of his own sin. Everyone in his family knew of his adultery with Bathsheba and his arrangement for her husband's death. His poor example of self-discipline may have kept him from being the father that his son desperately needed. As with every sinful father, David knew that his son could challenge his hypocrisy. "Who do you think *you* are?" Absalom could have rightly snapped at his father. So David was afraid to deal with his son, and as a result, he lost him forever.

Regardless of their personal sinfulness and failures, God has given fathers the privilege of being a leader to their children, of loving them ... of dealing directly with their rebellion. They have this charge, not from a platform of perfection, but from a call to be obedient.

Promises in Scripture

When your days are over and you rest with your fathers, I will raise up your offspring to succeed you, who will come from your own body, and I will establish his kingdom. He is the one who will build a house for my Name, and I will establish the throne of his kingdom forever. I will be his father, and he will be my son.

— 2 Samuel 7:12–14

Even though I walk
through the valley of the shadow of death,
I will fear no evil,
for you are with me;
your rod and your staff,
they comfort me.

— Psalm 23:4

Many are the woes of the wicked, but the LORD's
unfailing love
surrounds the man who trusts in him.

— Psalm 32:10

HIS LEGACY OF PRAYER

The LORD is my rock, my fortress and my deliverer;
*   my God is my rock, in whom I take refuge,*
*   my shield and the horn of my salvation.*
He is my stronghold, my refuge and my savior.
                                    —2 Samuel 22:2–3

Reflect On: 2 Samuel 22.

Praise God: For his promises.

Offer Thanks: For God's faithfulness in keeping his covenants.

Confess: The unconfessed sin that keeps you from serving God wholeheartedly.

Ask God: For a renewed willingness to follow him.

David's great song of praise gives credit where credit is due. It is a song that recounts God's faithful love in glorious detail, specifying all that God has done for him—saving him from violent men, drawing him out of deep waters, rescuing him from powerful enemies, and stooping down to make him great. It is the prayer of a man intimately familiar with the character of God.

David knew what the Lord was willing to do for the person who trusted in him. But instead of asking God to do something for you today, pray David's prayer of praise as though it is your own. Praise God in glorious detail for everything he has already done.

Lord, I will praise you for all the good you have done for me. For hearing my prayer and rescuing me. For lifting me up when I was in trouble. For blessing me in ways I could not have imagined. For defeating my enemies. For being my refuge and my shield. The Lord lives! Praise be to my Rock! Exalted be God, the Rock, my Savior! Amen.

JOB

❦

His Work: Job was a wealthy farmer, herdsman, and landowner.

His Children: Sons and daughters (all died), then seven sons and three daughters: Jemimah, Keziah, and Keren-Happuch

His Character: No one in the Old Testament carries a more remarkable résumé. "This man was blameless and upright; he feared God and shunned evil.... He was the greatest man among all the people of the East."

His Sorrow: Except for his own life and the life of his spouse, Job lost everything: cattle, camels, sheep, buildings, servants, and ten children. No one in all of Scripture—except Jesus—suffered more than he. Then to add to the physical devastation, Job had to endure the cross-examination and derision of three friends who clearly did not know what they were talking about.

His Triumph: In the end, Job was vindicated by the Lord, and God blessed him with more wealth than he had before. The Lord also gave him ten more children.

Key Scriptures: Job 1:2 – 40

HIS STORY

"Master, Master, Master ... something terrible has happened!"

The young messenger had never been so brazen. Ignoring protocol, he pushed back the servants and burst through the door into Job's private dining chamber.

Job stood and walked toward the panicked messenger. Grasping the young man's forearms with his hands, he tried to bring calm. But the man was inconsolable.

"The Sabeans ... they came to our fields ... they stole our livestock—the oxen, the donkeys ... and ... and they killed all the servants." Between gulps of air, the man told Job that he was the only one to survive. With these words, he collapsed against Job's chest and wept like a child.

Job held the messenger close, but his mind was in a whirl. *The Sabeans? I have no enemies among the Sabeans! What has provoked this attack? I must go and....* Before Job was able to finish the thought, another messenger came rushing into the room. His face and hands were black with soot, his clothes seared and reeking of smoke.

"Fire!" he shouted. "Fire has come from the heavens ... fire as I have never seen ... the skies opened and flames poured out onto our fields!"

"Tell me what you saw," Job commanded, his eyes fixed on the frantic man's face. "Tell me everything."

"Your sheep were grazing in the fields, my lord. There was a sound, like thunder ... but there were no clouds." The young man searched for words.

"Go on. Go on!" Job ordered, his voice rising to an uncommon level.

"Fire descended from heaven and destroyed the sheep, my lord. And the servants...." He paused as he realized what he was about to say. "Except for me, all the servants are dead." He began to cry. His body shook with sobs. Job drew the messenger to himself as the tears flowed.

Fire? Job's mind rifled through the possibilities. *Fire from the skies? How could this—*

Yet another messenger came running into his chambers, interrupting his thought. He told Job of the Chaldeans—some on foot, some on horseback, but all with weapons. "Three hordes of them descended on your fields, my lord. They slew all your camels and the servants that attended to them. I was the only one to escape."

"The Chaldeans?" Job bellowed. "What have I done to the Chal—"

Another messenger stormed into the room then, eyes glassy and face ashen. His lips were moving, but he made no sound. Surely there cannot be more bad news, Job thought. He stepped toward the panic-stricken man and grasped his shoulders, steeling himself for the worst.

"What is it?" Job asked the messenger, his voice hinting of a resigned calm. Inside, he already knew what was coming.

As if in a trance, the fourth messenger spoke evenly. "Your sons and daughters are dead." Job's hands fell from the man's shoulders. He did not speak. "A mighty wind came sweeping in from the desert," the messenger said. "The house collapsed on your children. They were crushed under the weight of the walls and the roof. No one survived. Only I was able to escape."

Job stood motionless. A grinding nausea formed in his stomach. His eyes were open, but nothing came into focus. Grasping his robe in both hands, he ripped the garment from top to bottom. He showed no anger. No rage. Only sorrow and unspeakable grief. And then suddenly Job's heart was filled with a strange sense of awe.

He called for his servants and ordered them to shave his head. Then, clearing the room, he fell to the ground in worship.

Naked I came from my mother's womb,
and naked I will depart.
The Lord gave and the Lord has taken away;
may the name of the LORD be praised.

A LOOK AT THE MAN

The Contest

It all seems so unfair. God and Satan climbed into opposing grandstands and thrust the unsuspecting Job into the arena.

"There is no one on earth like him," God asserted. "He is blameless and upright, a man who fears God and shuns evil."

"Of course he's faithful," Satan sneered. "Job's no fool. Look at what you've given him. Who wouldn't be upright with all that prosperity? He's got a good thing going." God knew exactly where this conversation was headed. He wrote the script before the earth was formed. "But open your hand and let me strike everything he has," Satan scoffed. "If I do this, he will curse you to your face. Destroy his things, and then we'll see how upright he is."

"Very well," God replied. "His possessions are all yours."

In that moment Job walked into the arena alone. And in less than a single day, he lost everything—five hundred yoke of oxen and five hundred donkeys, seven thousand sheep, and three thousand camels. In just a few hours, nearly all of Job's servants were dead, and then, in a final devastating blow, his seven sons and three daughters were destroyed in a tornado.

Job was broken yet steadfast.

But Satan was not ready to concede. "Open your hand and let me strike his body," Satan chortled to God. "No one can deal with that kind of pain. He will surely curse you to your face."

"Very well," God repeated. "His body is yours, but you may not kill him."

Then, just as Job was burying his last child, painful sores broke out over his entire body. From the top of his head to the bottom of his feet, he was covered with horrible wounds.

His wife had seen enough. "Are you still holding on to your God? What's the use?" she mocked. "Curse him and die!"

But Job refused. "Should we accept good from God and not trouble?"

Then three of Job's friends appeared. For one week they sat quietly with their suffering friend. Not a single word was spoken. At first their kindness opened Job's heart. Then it opened his mouth. He began the slow and downward spiral of asking "why?" "Why?" he asked one friend, shaking his head in disbelief. "Why?" he asked another, clinging to his hands. "Why?" he screamed at the sky. He cursed the day of his birth and expressed his longing to die.

Then Job and his three friends entered into a dialogue that lasted for many days. The conversation was deeply philosophical, tedious, and depressing. The words of Job's friends were neither comforting nor helpful.

"How long will you torment me and crush me with your words?" Job finally lamented.

Then God spoke to Job. "Brace yourself like a man," the Almighty began. "I will question you, and you shall answer me."

Job had never heard anything like this.

"Where were you when I laid the earth's foundations?" the sovereign God asked. "Tell me, if you understand, who marked off its dimensions? Surely you know!"

God's soliloquy continued uninterrupted. He exposed the greatness of his creation and the mystery and power of his being.

Job was stunned by God's words and overwhelmed by God's very presence amid his pain. "My ears had heard of you," Job finally said. "But now my eyes have seen you."

HIS LEGACY IN SCRIPTURE

Read Job 23

1. What is the world's view of suffering? What reasons do people give for suffering?
2. Find the words in this passage that underscore Job's deep loneliness. Tell about a time when you have had similar feelings.
3. Find the words in this passage that describe his ongoing love for God. How can suffering enhance our devotion to the Lord?

Going Deeper: Read Job 38:1–2

4. Job was enrolled in graduate school. His loss and pain were the tuition fees, and the conversations between himself, his friends, and God were his course work. These are the opening words of God's commencement address. What do you think they mean?

Read Job 42:1–3

5. These words represent Job's diploma. What do they mean?
6. What does Job's experience say to us today about suffering?

HIS LEGACY AS A FATHER

In a single day, Job lost his possessions—thus his liveli-hood—and his children ... and in a matter of a few days, his own health. How could a loving God allow a man who had been so upright to suffer like this? What was he really doing to Job—and why?

Toward the end of the story, we get a glimpse at the answer. God was asking Job a simple question: "Who are you, Job?"

As men, you and I are more often than not defined by the things that Job lost. When we meet a stranger, he may ask us about our career or where we live. If the questioning turns to our families, we take out a few photos of our wife and our children. Eventually the questions may turn to activities or sports we enjoy.

But such a conversation with Job would have been a short one. "My means of gainful employment is charred and smoldering," he would have groaned. "All my children are dead, and I am in such physical pain, it's all I can do to lie here in bed."

No longer was Job's identity defined by his surroundings. Symbolically, he stood before his Creator naked, broken, and alone.

God may allow suffering in our lives in order to draw his presence into sharp relief, shading out what we thought was more important than our relationship to him. With nothing to distract us, the stripping away of everything gives us a renewed appreciation for his perfect love and grace and his desire that we love and follow him without distraction.

In spite of how much we love our children and how important our role as their father may be, nothing can be more critical than the answer to his question: "Who are you?"

Our answer: "I am yours."

Promises in Scripture

Trouble and distress have come upon me,
but your commands are my delight.

—Psalm 119:143

Whoever trusts in his riches will fall,
but the righteous will thrive like a green leaf.

—Proverbs 11:28

Be joyful always; pray continually; give thanks in all circumstances, for this is God's will for you in Christ Jesus.

—1 Thessalonians 5:16–18

HIS LEGACY OF PRAYER

"Naked I came from my mother's womb,
    and naked I will depart.
The LORD gave and the LORD has taken away;
    may the name of the LORD be praised."

—Job 1:21

"My ears had heard of you
    but now my eyes have seen you."

—Job 42:5

Reflect On: Job 40:1–7.

Praise God: For this lesson graphically illustrated by his faithful servant.

Offer Thanks: For allowing us to draw closer to him no matter how painful our circumstances.

Confess: Our propensity to accuse God of unfairness when he allows suffering to come our way.

Ask God: To show you his perspective on your pain and your doubts and to grant you his peace — the peace that transcends understanding.

The two prayers above form bookends on Job's life. Job offers the first prayer soon after we meet him and the last near the end of the book. Like a boy maturing to manhood,

Job's love for God grows from simple praise—a very good thing—to intimacy—something even better.

Father, thank you for the life and example of Job. I praise you for his faithfulness in the face of suffering and pain. Please fill me with your Spirit so that I may learn from Job's faith—to love you, to praise you, to thank you, and to trust you in every circumstance, knowing that suffering can result in a deeper fellowship with you. I willingly submit to your direction in my life. I pray this in Jesus' name. Amen.

SOLOMON

His Name Means *Peaceable*

⌒◦◦◦⌒

His Children: Rehoboam, Basemath, Taphath

His Work: The son of King David and Bathsheba, Solomon was the third king of Israel.

His Character: Known until this day as the wisest man who ever lived.

His Sorrow: Although he was an extremely intelligent man, later in his life he became disobedient to God and sacrificed everything on the altar of sexual excess. His inability to lead his own children led to the kingdom's division and ultimate fall.

His Triumph: Solomon built the kingdom of Israel to its greatest level in material wealth and land.

Key Scriptures: 1 Kings 2–5

HIS STORY

Early in his reign as king, Solomon visited the city of Gibeon, not far from Jerusalem, to offer a sacrifice to the Lord. That night in a dream, God paid Solomon a visit of his own, and his invitation was stunning: "Ask for whatever you want me to give you."

Solomon stepped back in surprise. Just think of the possibilities, he thought to himself.

"You have shown great kindness to your servant, my father David," Solomon began thoughtfully, "because he was faithful to you and righteous and upright in heart. You have continued this great kindness to him and have given him a son to sit on his throne this very day.... But I am only a little child and do not know how to carry out my duties.... So give your servant a discerning heart to govern your people and to distinguish between right and wrong. For who is able to govern this great people of yours?"

"I will give you a wise and discerning heart," the Lord responded, "so that there will never have been anyone like you, nor will there ever be. Moreover, I will give you what you have not asked for—both riches and honor—so that in your lifetime you will have no equal among kings."

Solomon's eyes widened as his pulse quickened with wonder. Wisdom, riches, and honor—what else could a man hope for?

But then God added a sobering stipulation: "If you walk in my ways and obey my statutes and commands as David your father did, I will give you a long life." Solomon's face flushed in shame. He had already been disobedient. His first act as the king had been to take the daughter of the pharaoh of Egypt as his wife. But Solomon was moved by God's promise through his dream. When he returned to Jerusalem, he stood before the ark of the covenant and vowed his allegiance and obedience to the God of his father.

Soon God's provision of a wise and discerning heart was put to the test.

Two women stood before Solomon. "The living child is mine," one woman pled. Pointing to the other woman, she said, "It was she who rolled over in the night and smothered her child to death. Then, before I awoke, she gave me her dead child and took mine as her own."

"No, the living child is mine," the other woman demanded. "It was she who smothered her child."

"Bring me a sword," King Solomon commanded of his servants. "Now cut the living child in two and give half to one and half to the other."

The women — and all who were there — were shocked by the king's heartless plan.

"Please, my lord," cried one of the women. "Give her the living baby. Don't kill him!"

And with that, the king declared, "Give the living baby to the first woman. Do not kill him; she is his mother."

Even world-renowned dignitaries paid visits to Solomon. They came to see what he had accomplished and to test his wisdom with "hard questions." Such was the visit to Jerusalem by the queen of Sheba—a trip of almost twelve hundred miles. She arrived with a very great caravan—with camels carrying spices, large quantities of gold, and precious stones. The queen also came with all her questions. And, to her amazement, nothing was too hard for the king to explain to her.

Solomon accomplished many good things as Israel's third king. He orchestrated the building of a palace and the temple, a permanent house of worship and an apt dwelling place for the ark of the covenant. Built to elegant specifications, this holy building mirrored Solomon's love for God and his eye for beauty and attention to the smallest detail.

Politically, he organized the kingdom into twelve districts and appointed governors over each one. Educationally, Solomon held clinics and "described plant life, from the cedar of Lebanon to the hyssop that grew out of the walls. He also taught about animals and birds, reptiles and fish." A lover of the arts, Solomon spoke three thousand proverbs and his songs numbered a thousand and five.

But Solomon was a failure. His great accomplishments did not compensate for his unwillingness to "keep God's statutes." Solomon loved foreign women and had an insatiable appetite for them. In spite of God's specific instructions, the king married not one, but multiple women from neighboring countries. His rationale was that he was building coalitions with these nations. How could the Moabites, the Ammonites, the Edomites, the Hittites, and the Sidonians attack the Israelites when the population included their own daughters and grandchildren?

However, God's laws were clear. As a nation, Israel was young and vulnerable. Intermarrying with foreigners meant the unavoidable blending of their infant faith with pagan beliefs. God knew that his people—including someone as strong and wise as Solomon—would have a difficult time standing against these extraneous persuasions. He was right. And not only was Solomon to blame for not stopping this cancer, he was guilty of encouraging it.

Like Saul and David before him, God had recruited Israel's king from the ranks of mortal, sinful men. Saul's transgressions led to his destruction; David's led to contrition and repentance. With no legitimate excuse, Solomon did not follow David's example. Instead, like Saul, his flagrant disregard of God's laws led to his own spiritual destitution and death.

God's promise was clear: Obey me and live a long life. Disobey me and die.

In the end, Solomon's wisdom could not save him.

A LOOK AT THE MAN

The Legacy That Could Have Been

It's one of the most incredible moments in all of Scripture. The Lord of Israel, the Creator of the universe, makes an offer to a mortal man — Solomon, the son of David and the newly anointed king of Israel. Like the archetypal genie in the bottle, God asks Solomon to make a wish. But Solomon's historic opportunity becomes a vicious tragedy.

This may be the saddest story in the Bible.

It's the account of a man who literally had everything. The only thing more difficult to comprehend than his great mind, his enormous wealth and power were the prospects of what he could have done with these things. Solomon had the capability to change his world.

But in spite of doing many good things during his lifetime, he actually squandered this potential. Of course he built a name for himself. Go ahead and ask anyone to finish this sentence: "That guy over there has the wisdom of _____."

What happened to Solomon? The reason for his pathetic failure is no mystery. He broke this commandment: "You shall not make for yourself an idol in the form of anything in heaven above or on the earth beneath or in the waters below. You shall not bow down to them or worship them; for I, the LORD your God, am a jealous God" (Exodus 20:4–5).

Solomon should have known better. In fact, he did know better. As his father, David, was dying, Solomon heard these words. "Observe what the LORD your God requires: Walk in his ways, and keep his decrees and commands, his laws and requirements, as written in the Law of Moses, so that you may prosper in all you do and wherever you go."

But somehow Solomon believed he could be the exception to the rule, the one man who could break God's law without suffering the consequences. But God was not going to ignore all the idols and altars he had set up to please his foreign wives, accustomed as they were to worshiping various idols. Because of his infidelity, the kingdom of Israel split apart after his death, with Judah and its capital, Jerusalem, in the south and Israel and its capital, Samaria, in the north.

It was too late for Solomon to discover that a man before God's throne is judged by what is in his heart. "Set your affection on things above, not on things on the earth" (Colossians 3:2 KJV).

Instead of leaving a world-changing legacy, Solomon leaves us with a graphic lesson in eternal fruitlessness—with no excuses.

HIS LEGACY IN SCRIPTURE

Read 1 Kings 3:5–15

1. God appears to Solomon and invites him to ask for anything he wants. What does the new king's response reveal about his character? What does the Lord's response reveal about God?

2. If God made the same invitation to you, what would you ask for?

Read 1 Kings 8:10–11, 27–30

3. Why was it so important for Solomon to build a temple?

4. Why do you think Solomon acknowledges that God cannot be contained in a physical place despite clear evidence that God is dwelling in the temple he has built?

Read 1 Kings 11:1–13

5. Even though he experiences a life of tremendous blessing, Solomon strays from God and falls into the sin of idolatry. How does the condition of his heart deteriorate over time?

6. How can prosperity be dangerous to your spiritual health?

Interesting Fact

God inspired King David with the pattern for the temple, which he passed on to Solomon. Because the entire building and everything in it was ordained by God, no detail of its construction was considered insignificant. For instance, 1 Kings 6 describes carvings of cherubim and beautiful trees and flowers on the doors leading to the inner sanctuary. These were to remind the Israelites of the Garden of Eden, the paradise from which Adam and Eve were ejected because of their sin. The carved, olive wood doors symbolized the way back to paradise through the atonement for sin made in the sanctuary of the temple.

HIS LEGACY AS A FATHER

Solomon will forever be remembered as Israel's wisest king. And, no doubt, he would have bragged about how bright his children were as well. But wise father Solomon didn't leave anything to chance; he didn't just figure that his children would pick up his wisdom on their own.

The book of Proverbs is, actually, a love note to Solomon's children. Wise and wealthy as he was, he saw the value of training children "for attaining wisdom and discipline ... for acquiring a disciplined and prudent life, doing what is right and just and fair" (Proverbs 1:2–3). Solomon stopped and took the time to pour wisdom into his children. As a result of his efforts, men and women throughout history have basked in the glow of his wise words.

Unfortunately, Solomon's wisdom came to a screeching halt when it came to his own behavior, and this had a predictable affect on his effectiveness as a father. "Don't do as I do, do as I say," is less debilitating to a man's legacy centuries after he's gone than it is when he's standing in front of his children.

Today we marvel at Solomon's insight and brilliance in Proverbs, but his sons and daughters must have marveled at his inability to do what he challenged others to do. As is so often true about children who watch their fathers, they weren't as impressed with his words as they were by his life.

Promises in Scripture

Your house and your kingdom will endure forever before me; your throne will be established forever.

—2 Samuel 7:16

Praise be to the LORD, *who has given rest to his people Israel just as he promised. Not one word has failed of all the good promises he gave.*

—1 Kings 8:56

For to us a child is born,
*   to us a son is given,*
*   and the government will be on his shoulders.*
And he will be called
*   Wonderful Counselor, Mighty God,*
*   Everlasting Father, Prince of Peace.*
Of the increase of his government and peace
*   there will be no end.*

—Isaiah 9:6–7

HIS LEGACY OF PRAYER

Your hearts must be fully committed to the LORD our God, to live by his decrees and obey his commands."

— 1 Kings 8:61

Reflect On: 1 Kings 8:56–61; 11:9–13.

Praise God: For his constancy. He is the same yesterday, today, and forever.

Offer Thanks: That God's words are consistent with his character.

Confess: Any wavering in your devotion to God.

Ask God: To help you maintain a course that will daily bring you closer to him.

It's called drift. Strong currents pull you west when you intend to go east or north when you want to head south. It happens when you either fail to notice or fail to make timely course corrections to maintain your heading. Remember the old saying, "The road to hell is paved with good intentions"? That's exactly what can happen to a person whose heart has drifted away from God. Perhaps the person started with the best of intentions. But intentions are so easy, so pleasant to entertain. Good ones make us feel good about ourselves.

The hard part is staying the course, resisting the temptation to let personal desires or circumstances push you off course. Drift is what happened to Solomon. His heart drifted from complete devotion to God to a halfhearted devotion. He wanted God, but he wanted other things as well—powerful alliances, beautiful women, other gods. And so his kingdom drifted away from God. Today, pray for the grace to recognize whatever drift has occurred in your own life. Ask God to anchor you more completely in him. If you need to change course, ask for the wisdom and courage to do whatever it takes to get back on track with him.

Father in heaven, Solomon warned the people to "fully commit" their hearts to you. And then he failed to take his own advice. Help me to recognize any drift that has occurred in my life. Restore the deepest desires of my heart, the ones you have put there. Bring me back to you and give me a stronger resolve to do whatever it takes to remain faithful. In Jesus' name, Amen.

JOSEPH

His Name Means *May He [God] Add*

✦

His Children: Jesus, James, Joseph, Simon, Judas, and unnamed daughters[1]

His Work: Joseph was a working man who supported his family through the trade of carpentry.

His Character: A man who traced his ancestry back to David, Joseph was just, compassionate, and obedient to God. Though poor, he was a good husband and father, providing for and protecting his family.

His Sorrow: That Herod the Great tried to murder his son, Jesus.

His Triumph: To be used by God to protect and provide for the world's Savior. Through him, Jesus could trace his ancestry to King David and the tribe of Judah.

Key Scriptures: Matthew 1–2; Luke 2

HIS STORY

Joseph had no complaints. Nazareth kept a carpenter of his skill and reputation as busy as he cared to be, making plows, yokes, roofs, doors, and window shutters. He loved the smell and heft of the wood, the unique pattern and possibility of each board hewn from the greenwood. Once dried, the oak planks were sturdy and reliable, like the man himself.

Working alone in his workshop gave Joseph time to think and to remember. He recalled a day more than twelve years earlier that had almost shattered him, the day he discovered that Mary, the woman he had been engaged to, had become pregnant. Strangely, Joseph had felt no rage, only a great disappointment that settled like a permanent knot in his chest, weighing him down with the deepest sadness. How could his judgment have been so flawed, so far from the mark? He had looked forward to marrying the young woman whose character and temperament had made her seem all the more likable.

Rather than dragging her before the elders, Joseph had decided to divorce Mary quietly. Her life would be hard enough without a husband, and he had no need to watch her suffer publicly for what she had done. But before he had the chance to carry out his plan, Joseph had a dream. In it he saw an angel who told him, "Joseph son of David, do not be afraid to take Mary home as your wife, because what is conceived in her is from the Holy Spirit. She will give birth to a son, and you are to give him the name Jesus, because he will save his people from their sins." Rather than brushing off the dream as a product of the previous night's meal, Joseph took it to heart, bringing Mary home as his wife.

But before they could settle in, Caesar Augustus ordered every man in his vast empire to register in a census. For Joseph, that meant traveling south to Bethlehem, the city of David, his ancestral home. But would Mary, now several months pregnant, be strong enough for the trip, he wondered. Perhaps he should leave her in Nazareth in the care of her family. But that would expose her to all the mean-spirited gossip already circulating about her pregnancy. No, he could not bear to part with his wife.

So the couple set out for Bethlehem, finding the roads jammed with people hurrying to comply with the census. The closer they came to the town, the more worried Joseph became. With so little money and so many people on the move, how would he find a place for them to stay? Once in the city, his fears seemed justified as house after house refused them.

"Sorry, we're full."

"Try the inn down the street, why don't you?"

"I feel bad about your wife, buddy, but we're already packed so tight we can hardly breathe."

In the small town of Bethlehem, the city of David, there was no room for Joseph, no room for his wife, and no room for the child who was to be born — the one the angel had said would save the people from their sins.

Finally, someone told Joseph about a cave full of animals. At least it was dry, it would keep the wind off for a while, and it would cost little. Sweeping out a corner of the cave, the couple lined the ground with blankets and hay and then unpacked their few provisions.

Exhausted from the journey, they at last had a place to lay their heads, a place where Mary could give birth. When her labor was finally over, she wrapped the baby in long strips of cloth to keep him warm and then handed him to Joseph. Awkwardly at first, he took the boy, brushing a large finger-tip across the small lips, the perfect nose, the wrinkled brow. Then he hugged the baby to his chest, feeling a strange sense of pride, a fierce love rising up in him. What a thing of won-der this child was — his son to cherish and protect.

The next night, Joseph was surprised to see strangers ap-proaching the cave. He could tell by the look and smell of the ragtag bunch that they must be shepherds. One of the men stepped forward eagerly, deferentially. "We want to see the baby, sir." Craning his neck as if to see through the shadows, the man pointed. "Is that him there?"

Joseph invited the men inside. But how had they heard about the child, and why were they so agitated? He didn't have long to wait for an explanation, because each man was eager to share his version of what had taken place.

"We were minding our sheep out in the field," one man piped up.

"Suddenly the whole sky lit up," said another.

"I fell on my face because I thought it was the end of the world," said the roughest of the bunch.

"Even the sheep fell over." They all laughed as they re-called the scene, though no one had laughed at the time.

Joseph and Mary listened carefully as the shepherds told them about the glorious angel who had tried to calm them by saying, "Do not be afraid. I bring you good news of great joy that will be for all the people. Today in the town of David a Savior has been born to you; he is Christ the Lord. This will be a sign to you: You will find a baby wrapped in cloths and lying in a manger." Then more angels had come, praising God and saying: "Glory to God in the highest, and on earth peace to men on whom his favor rests."

In the time that followed, Joseph had more strange encounters—an old man and an old woman in the temple in Jerusalem; Magi following a star from the east; an angel warning him in a dream to take the boy and his mother and flee to Egypt; another angel telling him when it was safe to return home. What it all meant, Joseph did not know for certain. He only knew how glad he felt to be the father of this boy and the husband of this woman. Surely the holy God who had cared for them so well would continue to watch over his Son, the One who was to inherit the throne of David and save his people from their sins.

A LOOK AT THE MAN

Everything a Father Should Be

Three times Joseph saw angels in his dreams. In the first appearance, the angel announced something impossible: Mary had become pregnant, though she had not been unfaithful to him. In the second, the angel warned him to flee to Egypt to escape Herod's plan to murder the boy Jesus. Later, an angel sounded the all clear, informing Joseph of Herod's death so that he could return to Israel with Mary and Jesus.

Though we know little of Joseph from the Scriptures, we know at least of his remarkable faith and obedience. Each time the angels appeared to him, they revealed something he could not have known without divine revelation. But each new revelation presented him with a choice. Would he do as the angel instructed, or would he rely on his own understanding and do as he thought best?

It would have been so easy to brush off the first dream. When in the history of the world had a woman ever become pregnant without sleeping with a man? Common sense would have told him to proceed with his plan to set Mary aside and marry someone else. Instead, he heeded the angel and, by doing so, said yes to God's surprising plan for his life.

Did Joseph comprehend the enormity of the decisions he was making? Possibly. But certainly he could not foresee the strange mixture of blessing and suffering that lay in store for him and his family. His yes would cost him many sleepless nights, but it would also involve him in the greatest miracle ever.

Centuries later we celebrate Joseph's life, knowing that he was everything a father should be—spiritually perceptive, compassionate, humble, faithful, loving, and protective toward the family the Lord had given him.

HIS LEGACY IN SCRIPTURE

Read Matthew 1:18–21

1. As a carpenter, Joseph was a man with physical strength. But what do these verses tell us about the strength of Joseph's character?
2. Even more painful than the news that Mary was pregnant by someone other than himself was the knowledge that he had been betrayed. How would you feel if you were in Joseph's situation?
3. What did Joseph have the right to do? What did he decide to do? What were his motives?

Important Fact

Joseph was the earthly father of Jesus, the Messiah. God had chosen Mary to be the mother of the Savior, and God had chosen Joseph to take this very important role in the life of the growing boy.

Read Ephesians 6:1–4

4. Fathers are told not to exasperate or provoke their children to anger. How do they frustrate their children?
5. Fathers are to bring their children up in the training and instruction of the Lord. What specific things should you do to obey this admonition?

HIS LEGACY AS A FATHER

Over the years, many have wondered how conscious Jesus was of his messiahship. How closely did his childhood resemble that of an ordinary youngster living in Nazareth?

Regardless of the answer to this question, it's clear that, like any young man, his earthly father had a profound impact on him. In fact, one of the most remarkable things about Joseph is that God purposefully selected him from many possible candidates to be a living example for his young son and apprentice.

"Who will set an example for my Son?" God may have wondered. "Who will love him completely, teach him patiently, discipline him gently, and model for him what a man after my heart looks like?"

In his providence, God chose Joseph, the carpenter from Nazareth. A direct descendant of King David, another man after God's own heart, Joseph was selected for this incredible assignment.

Years before he was recognized as — or confessed to being — the Son of God, the Savior of the world, Jesus was known as "the son of Joseph." This puts Joseph, the man teaching his boy a carpenter's trade, in a category all by himself.

Promises in Scripture

If ... you seek the LORD your God, you will find him if you look for him with all your heart and with all your soul.

— Deuteronomy 4:29

Be strong and very courageous. Be careful to obey all the law my servant Moses gave you; do not turn from it to the right or to the left, that you may be successful wherever you go.

— Joshua 1:7

Humility and the fear of the LORD
bring wealth and honor and life.

— Proverbs 22:4

You did not choose me, but I chose you and appointed you to go and bear fruit — fruit that will last. Then the Father will give you whatever you ask in my name.

— John 15:16

HIS LEGACY OF PRAYER

An angel of the Lord appeared to Joseph in a dream....
So he got up, took the child and his mother during the night and
left for Egypt.

—Matthew 2:13–14

An angel of the Lord appeared in a dream to Joseph in Egypt....
So he got up, took the child and his mother and went to the land
of Israel.

—Matthew 2:19, 21

Reflect On: Genesis 39:1–5. (This is an account of another Joseph, but the similarities between
these two obedient men and God's gracious
blessing is striking.)

Praise God: For offering a love that constrains us to
obedience.

Offer Thanks: For blessing you with the responsibility of
leading and directing the lives of young
people—children, nieces, nephews, grandchildren, neighbors.

Confess: Your sin and willful disobedience.

Ask God: To give you a heart that is drawn to him in
love and compliance to his perfect will and

to empower you in the task of leading these young ones in his ways.

In the Gospels, Jesus challenges his disciples with the words, "From everyone who has been given much, much will be demanded; and from the one who has been entrusted with much, much more will be asked" (Luke 12:48). Joseph was entrusted with the responsibility of raising the eternal Son of God. What an incredible charge! But never forget, every child is a miraculous gift and every parent's responsibility is a sobering one.

Father, thank you for calling great men like Joseph to be your servants. Thank you for entrusting him with your blessed Son as you have entrusted me with those under my care. Lord, please grant me wisdom and understanding. I confess my sins and ask that you draw me to yourself by your mercy. Make me a worthy ambassador of your love. In Jesus' name I humbly pray, Amen.

THE PRODIGAL SON, THE ELDER BROTHER, AND THEIR FATHER

⸛

Their Work: The father was a wealthy landowner and his sons worked for him.

Their Character: Although it may have been based on a real family, Jesus told this story as a parable. His point was to draw a word picture of what a loving and forgiving father looked like. Both of the brothers were sinners. One committed the sin of unrighteous living and the other the sin of self-righteousness.

Their Sorrow: Both of the sons were alienated from their father. Geography separated the prodigal from his father, while pride separated the elder brother.

Their Triumph: The father's open arms and homecoming feast welcomed the prodigal. There was no happiness for the elder brother except the misplaced belief that he was better than his wayward sibling.

Key Scripture: Luke 15

THEIR STORY

"Father," the young man called.

"Yes, my son," the old man eagerly replied. Conversations between the two were infrequent and strained these days. But any hopes for a meaningful talk were dashed by his son's next words.

"I don't want to wait for you to die in order to receive my inheritance," the boy said with his defiant chin upraised. "I want you to give it to me now."

Inwardly, his son's words staggered the father. Insolent child! How could he say such a thing? Hurt but unwilling to challenge the incorrigible lad, he numbly retrieved the money and handed it to his son. He wished that he could warn the boy not to squander his inheritance. *I don't want to see him throw away his future*, he thought. There was so much that could destroy the young man. But knowing his son would merely ignore his warnings, the father said nothing.

The father watched him—a child he had held within minutes of his birth, a child he had cherished from that day forward—disappear without a backward glance down the road that led from the family home.

When the boy's older brother heard what he had done, he was furious. "How could you do such a thing?" he said, scolding his father. "You know what he will do with the money. And you also know," the brother added, "that soon he'll come back to you for more."

The father was silent, hoping that the older brother was right. He longed to see his son again, whatever the conditions. Before long, word of the young man's exploits—and his apparent pleasure—reached home, grieving the father all the more.

Meanwhile the boy was having the time of his life. Not only did a pocketful of money buy him all the pleasure and happiness he could want, but he found himself surrounded with the kind of fast-moving friends he had always wished for. No more sleepy farmers. No more dull herdsmen. No more plain and simple female neighbors. This was better than he had imagined.

But soon the young man's fingers touched the bottom of his money pouch. He couldn't believe how quickly the money had vanished. *Now what will I do?* he wondered. *I have no skills for a worthwhile trade.* With mute shock he watched his newfound friends disappear.

Responding to news that a local pig farmer had an opening for a hired hand, the lonely, desperate boy landed a job slopping hogs. Day after day he cared for the pigs. And day after day his spirits sank. Then one morning the son came to his senses. "What am I doing here?" he asked the swine, as though he expected them to answer. "At least I would be able to eat better than this if I were working for my father." The pigs did not look up from their breakfast. "I will go home and offer to be one of my father's servants."

But would his father have him? How horribly the boy had treated him! He had not honored his father or loved him. Instead, he had lived in a way that denied everything his father had taught him. Would his father ever forgive him?

The thought of being turned away set the son's hands to trembling.

What kind of future would he have without a father? Without a home? "What have I done?" he cried.

Late one afternoon, while absently staring out a window, the boy's father saw something in the distance that surprised him—a tiny figure advancing against the horizon in the exact place he had last seen his son. As the figure grew closer, the father wondered, *Could it be? No! Certainly not! But it looks like ...* The young man's gait was noticeably slower, his shoulders stooped.... But make no mistake about it, it was his boy. He was home!

Without hesitation the father ran down the road toward his son, his arms outstretched and his robes flagging in his wake.

When the young man looked up and saw the man running toward him, his knees buckled. He knew who this was. What punishment would his father exact? Whipping? Exile? Pure contrition was his only chance for survival.

"O Father," the boy wept as his father reached him, "I have sinned against God and against you. I do not deserve to be your ..."

But the man was not listening. "Good news! Good news!" He shouted so loudly that the neighbors could hear. He lifted his shocked son from his knees, pulling him into his arms, laughing and shouting. Servants in the field gawked at them, but his father paid them no heed. "Kill the fatted calf! Break out the wine. We're going to have a homecoming feast tonight." The father took his son's face between his hands and grinned until his son gazed back at him. "My son who was lost has been found." And then he embraced him again.

This time the son clung to his father as eagerly as the father did to his son.

"What's the commotion?" the elder brother asked his servants when he returned from a long day of toiling in the fields. "What's all the noise—the music and the laughter?"

"It's your younger brother, my lord," they answered. "He is home, and your father is throwing a party in his honor."

Shaking his head in disbelief, his body trembling with fury, the brother stormed to the receiving room of his father. "What are you doing?" he shouted. "Who is this scoundrel that he deserves your forgiveness, much less a celebration? Haven't you done enough for that rascal?"

And then, as though it was an afterthought, he added, "After all I have done for you—and you treat me like this?"

But the father ignored the elder brother's churlishness. His heart had never been this full of gratitude and love ... for both of his sons.

"My dear son," the father said to his eldest child, "you have been with me always, and I thank you for that. But don't keep me from celebrating your brother's return. Come to the party," he pleaded. "Please come and celebrate."

But the elder brother turned and walked away. The injustice! How could this be fair? How could his father be so blind? He would not join in such revelry over someone who deserved so little—not even at the request of his father.

A LOOK AT THE MEN

The Unrighteous and the Self-Righteous

This biblical account is one of Jesus' parables, often called "The Story of the Prodigal Son." But it's really the story of not one but three men: the prodigal son, the elder brother, and the waiting father. Each plays a critical role in the narrative.

What the younger son asked of his father was unthinkable. Inheritance was paid to a man's sons upon his death, so in prematurely requesting the birthright from his father, the boy was saying that he wouldn't care if his father were dead. His rebellion was open and shameless, a public embarrassment for the entire family. And what he did broke his father's heart.

The older boy was every father's dream. As an employee, his efforts were productive, his work ethic was flawless. Even his conduct was exemplary—and he did not hesitate to review all of these qualities in his father's hearing. He had every confidence that his virtuous behavior earned not only his father's respect and riches but his love as well.

But the elder brother carried a deep grudge. The insolence of his younger brother's words and the slack in his life ground away at the elder brother's soul like a millstone. And the special attention the young son drew from the father turned the older son's grudge into hatred.

As far as the elder brother was concerned, the moment the inheritance payment was made to his sibling, the boy's days as a member of the family were finished. Now the older son was his father's only son, and the benefits of his father's wealth would be exclusively his.

Unfortunately for the elder brother, this was not his father's disposition. The younger son, even with his inheritance paid in full, was still a member of the family. Neither open defiance nor running away would have any effect on his father's love for him. This infuriated the elder brother, but his simmering anger was about to be turned into a bubbling cauldron.

The father threw a party.

It was bad enough for his absent little brother to keep their father in distress while he was in a faraway land, but to have his father throw a celebration when he returned home was more than the elder brother could bear. In his attempt to punish the father for his grace, the elder brother refused to attend the merrymaking, preferring to sulk instead.

In this parable Jesus was declaring all of humankind "sinners," and he divided them into two groups: prodigals and elder brothers—the unrighteous and the self-righteous. And he underscored the fact that the heavenly Father—the living God—loved both and was willing to forgive both.

Contrition for his blatant sinfulness earned the younger brother full forgiveness and a party in his honor. But the older son's inability to see his self-righteousness as sin kept him from receiving the forgiveness his father would have freely extended. So he spent the night alone, overhearing the joyous celebration but experiencing none of it himself.

THEIR LEGACY IN SCRIPTURE

Read Luke 15:11–32

1. If you had been the father, which of the sons would you have been tempted to love more? Why?

2. Which son did it seem the father in the story loved more? Why?

3. The story of the three men is recorded in twenty-one verses (vv. 11–32). Almost half of these verses (vv. 25–32) tell us about the elder brother. Why do you think Jesus spends this much time talking about him?

Read Luke 15:1–3

4. To whom does Jesus tell the three stories found in Luke 15? Why is this an important clue as to the shameless sins of the prodigal and the hidden transgressions of the elder brother?

Going Deeper: Read Luke 15:4–10

5. The first of these stories is about a lost sheep. How did the sheep get lost? What did the shepherd do when he realized the sheep was lost?

6. The second story is about a lost coin. How did the coin get lost? What did the woman do when she realized the coin was lost?

7. The third story is about a lost son. How did the son get lost? What did the father do when he realized his son was lost?

Additional Thought

There is a sidelight to this story that may be helpful in understanding and healing relationships. When someone wanders off (the lost sheep) or when someone is misplaced — or damaged — by another person's carelessness (the lost coin), aggressive pursuit is advisable. But when a person defiantly rebels and gets lost by his own hand (the lost boy), the appropriate response is to love and wait. Intentional pursuit carries with it the liability that this lost person will be driven further away.

A LEGACY OF A FATHER AND HIS SONS

Although Jesus' account may have been based on a true story, these are nameless and fictional characters. But it doesn't matter. Because what Jesus does in telling this parable is to attach one of three names to every one of us: prodigal son or elder brother … or waiting father.

Jesus reminds us, and those who were listening to him that day, "God is your loving father. His mercy is completely reliable, his grace is abundant and free." The Master also uses this story to tell us that we can be divided into two categories — the unrighteous and the self-righteous. (Notice that "sinless" wasn't one of his choices.)

The "tax collectors and 'sinners'" knew that they were the prodigal. Their sin had been deliberate and visible. But the "Pharisees and teachers of the law" were the elder brother — and proud of it. They weren't interested in confessing anything, and so, according to the Teacher, they weren't eligible to come to the party.

Promises in Scripture

Do not worry, saying, "What shall we eat?" or "What shall we drink?" or "What shall we wear?" For the pagans run after all these things, and your heavenly Father knows that you need them. But seek first his kingdom and his righteousness, and all these things will be given to you as well.

— Matthew 6:31 – 33

This righteousness from God comes through faith in Jesus Christ to all who believe. There is no difference, for all have sinned and fall short of the glory of God, and are justified freely by his grace through the redemption that came by Christ Jesus.

— Romans 3:22 – 24

[Christ] had to be made like his brothers in every way, in order that he might become a merciful and faithful high priest in service to God, and that he might make atonement for the sins of the people. Because he himself suffered when he was tempted, he is able to help those who are being tempted.

— Hebrews 2:17 – 18

THEIR LEGACY OF PRAYER

"This son of mine was dead and is alive again; he was lost and is found." So they began to celebrate.

—Luke 15:24

Reflect On: Luke 15:20–31.

Praise God: For his mercy.

Offer Thanks: For the picture of the waiting father and how it tells us of the loving heavenly Father, who is eager to forgive our sins of unrighteousness and self-righteousness.

Confess: Any tendency to believe that good deeds earn us a place in the kingdom.

Ask God: To change your attitude, to give you a compassion for the lost, and to make your obedience to him a response to his love rather than treating it as a way to earn his love.

The story of the prodigal and the elder brother is the story of sin, repentance, and the loving father. Although the prodigal's sin of unrighteousness is far more visible than the elder brother's sin of self-righteousness, they are equally wicked in the father's eyes. And they keep us from the celebration that comes from having a clean heart.

Scripture makes it clear that it is not by our works but by Jesus' blood and righteousness that we are made right before a holy God. Our attempts at righteousness will fail. Holiness can only be a gift we receive from God.

Father in heaven, I confess my sinfulness. Thank you for the gift of forgiveness. Thank you that you place no higher value on self-righteousness than unrighteousness. Forgive me for believing that my good deeds make me better than my lost brother. Please give me a repentant heart so that I may experience the joy of my salvation. I pray this in Jesus' name, Amen.

NOTE

1. Some Christians, notably Catholics, believe that Jesus did not have blood siblings. They argue for this position on the fact that the Greek word *adelphos*, translated as "brothers," can also be used to designate other close relations like half-brothers, step-brothers, nephews, or cousins.

We want to hear from you. Please send your comments about this book to us in care of zreview@zondervan.com. Thank you.

GRAND RAPIDS, MICHIGAN 49530 USA

ZONDERVAN.COM/
AUTHORTRACKER